PRAISE FOR
THE FIVE LESSONS A MILLIONAIRE TAUGHT ME ABOUT LIFE AND WEALTH

"This book is a must-read for everyone seeking prosperity through correct financial principles."

—GARY TERAN, president, First Western Advisors

"The dependence on the illusionary benefits of money is bankrupting the hearts and financial lives of Americans. It is critical that we rethink our beliefs, actions, and relationships with money. Is it too late to think differently and make better choices? Evans's answer is a resounding no. The five lessons are a timely blessing that should be instilled into our beliefs and, most important, our hearts. I highly recommend everyone read this book."

—BOB BROOKS, *The Prudent Money Show*

"The educational void we have in this country when it comes to money and investing is exposed and examined well in *The Five Lessons.* But Richard Paul Evans makes sure that we don't forget the importance of generosity and kindness to go along with success. . . . This book is a gift of knowledge for anyone looking for the right path to both monetary and spiritual health."

—GARY GOLDBERG, *Money Matters Financial Network*

"This book underscores years of proven lessons I've passed to listeners and clients. I knew it hit the mark after one of my most influential and successful clients called me to say that he passed the book to his grandchildren as a good guide to lessons in life."

—STUART L. STEIN, *Your Estate Matters* radio program

"Oliver Wendell Holmes taught, 'I wouldn't give a fig for the simplicity on this side of complexity, but I would give my right arm for the simplicity on the far side of complexity.' These five lessons represent that simplicity with a larger sublime context."

—DR. STEPHEN R. COVEY,
author of *The 7 Habits of Highly Effective People*

"Richard Paul Evans not only teaches the prudent acquisition of wealth but the proper way to use it. I would as readily recommend this book to the young, cash-strapped newlywed couple as to the manager of a multibillion-dollar enterprise."

—ROBERT C. GAY, managing director, Bain Capital

"In *The Five Lessons a Millionaire Taught Me About Life and Wealth,* Richard Paul Evans explains in a concise and, therefore, powerful way the principles of wealth. You, who are willing to put the Five Lessons into practice, will become wealthy. And in doing so, you will increase your powers of opportunity and your ability to be generous in a faltering world."

—HYRUM SMITH, cofounder, Franklin Covey

THE FIVE

LESSONS A

MILLIONAIRE

TAUGHT ME

for Women

#1 *New York Times* bestselling author

Richard Paul Evans

Author of *The Five Lessons a Millionaire Taught Me
About Life and Wealth*

A Fireside Book
Published by Simon & Schuster
New York   London   Toronto   Sydney

Adapted from *The Five Lessons a Millionaire Taught Me About Life and Wealth*. Portions of this book were first published in *The Five Lessons a Millionaire Taught Me About Life and Wealth*.

Fireside
A Division of Simon & Schuster, Inc.
1230 Avenue of the Americas
New York, NY 10020

First Fireside hardcover edition January 2009

Fireside and colophon are registered trademarks of Simon & Schuster, Inc.

For information about special discounts for bulk purchases, please contact Simon & Schuster Special Sales at 1-800-456-6798 or business@simonandschuster.com.

Designed by Elliott Beard

Manufactured in the United States of America

10   9   8   7   6   5   4   3   2

Library of Congress Cataloging-in-Publication Data
Evans, Richard Paul.
   The five lessons a millionaire taught me for women / Richard Paul Evans.
       p.   cm.
   1. Women—Finance, Personal. 2. Finance, Personal. 3. Women—Life skills guides. I. Title
HG179.E893   2009
332.0240082—dc22   2008053008

ISBN-13: 978-1-4516-9185-6

To my true wealth—Jenna, Allyson, Abigail, McKenna, and Michael.

ACKNOWLEDGMENTS

I am very grateful for all those who helped make this book possible. First, to all the women who have shared with me their stories, successes, and hurts. Karen Roylance, my writing assistant, for her dedication, ideas, and insight. To my Five Lessons Institute team: Meagen Bunten, Karen Christoffersen, Barry Evans, Marc Steele (and his team), Chrystal Hodges, Judy Schiffman, and Laurie Liss. To Miche Barbosa, for taking such good care of me. To our 5 Lessons CRs, for your passion and hard work. (Especially you, Troy, Pamela, and Mo.) Also, Barney and Bonnie Hellenbrand at HBW. To my "Giving Back" team: Lisa Johnson and Lisa McDonald. And a special thanks to Mark Gompertz, Zachary Schisgal, and the folks at Fireside who, seeing the need, brought this book to market in record time.

Of course, thank you to my mentor, Kerry Heinz, for helping out a twelve-year-old boy who was down on his luck.

CONTENTS

Contents

Dear Reader,

Before you read this book there are five things you deserve to know.

1. I Wrote *The Five Lessons* to Make *You* Rich, Not Me.

I believe that most get-rich books are written to make the author rich. I didn't want my readers to think that about my book and to possibly discount its message. I solved this problem by giving away *all* my author royalties from *The Five Lessons* to help abused children. I will continue to give away my author royalties from this book as well.

2. The Story of My Millionaire Mentor Is True.

My millionaire mentor, Kerry Heinz, taught me these powerful lessons when I was a twelve-year-old boy. Though Mr. Heinz is now retired, I am fortunate that my relationship with this wonderful man and his family continues to this day.

3. The Principles in This Book Work in Good Times *and* Bad.

In fact, they work exceptionally well in both. I've spent a lifetime proving them. I've also heard from women around the world whose lives have been changed by these principles. The foreword to this book, written by my niece Heather, is a great example of how powerfully these principles can work. If you follow them, you will see financial change in your life, likely much faster than you expect.

4. The Acquisition of Money Is a Psychological Process.

These Five Lessons work so well because they take into account natural psychological tendencies. The fact that these principles are simple to follow does not make them less effective. The simplicity of the process *is* its genius.

5. Like You, I've Also Made Financial Mistakes.

I think I've made every mistake I write about in this book. Every time I stepped from the path of the Five Lessons I paid for it. Literally. My mistakes have only proven to me the importance and efficacy of these lessons. May you wisely learn from my mistakes instead of your own.

In the course of writing a book for women I encountered two primary difficulties. First, no definition of a specific social group will apply to all of its members. Ever. There are exceptions in every group. In money matters there are women who are financial geniuses and those who struggle to balance their checkbook. In writing this book I decided to reach women at the most basic level to help as many as possible.

Second, the ability to substantiate usable research was often hampered by people or groups with political agendas. Not surprisingly, I frequently came across contradictory reports about women's financial trends. This book isn't a political treatise. The sole purpose and agenda of this book is to help women succeed financially. Period. In these difficult economic times and with the challenges women face today, nothing could be more important.

In the face of contradictory information, I have chosen to rely on my personal observations and research. Over the past three years I've had the privilege of sharing the Five Lessons with thousands of women. I've heard their stories firsthand and read about their experiences through letters and e-mails. I've personally mentored groups of women for months at a time. I have an entire notebook filled with personal financial anecdotes sent in by women. The composite of these experiences has helped me paint a picture of where women are in the financial world. Not every woman, but the majority of them.

One of the beneficial results of my interactions is that I've identified five mistakes women frequently make when it comes to money. These include:

Unenlightened Beliefs About Money
Undervaluing Their Assets
"Burnt Toast Syndrome"
Investment Paralysis
Overtrusting

This book contains proven solutions for each of these problems. **Every principle in this book has been tested by women.** I've seen, firsthand, these principles dramatically change women's attitudes and lives. As the father of four daughters, I have a vested interest in helping women live better, happier, and more fulfilling lives. That's my sincere hope for you.

Good fortune in your new life,
Richard

Heather McVey

It's hard to believe that just a few years ago my life was so different. Or so painful. Financially, I was in a downward spiral that showed no sign of turning around. *How did I get here?* was a question that was constantly on my mind. *Where did we go wrong?*

My name is Heather McVey and I am Richard Paul Evans's niece. And, I might add, if it wasn't for me you probably wouldn't be reading about the Five Lessons, because my story was one of the reasons for the original book. When I saw, firsthand, the power of these lessons and experienced the joy and freedom these lessons brought, I urged my uncle to share these five secrets with everyone around the world.

They say turnabout is fair play, so as he wrote the original *Five Lessons* book he came back and asked me to share my story. My immediate response was "No way!" It was too embarrassing. I didn't want people to know how bad our financial situation had been. I'm glad I changed my mind.

We were probably not too different from you, trying to

raise our family and working hard to make ends meet. My success with living the Five Lessons completely changed my life. And if sharing my story would inspire just one person to experience the joy we've found, then I had to share. I'm pleased to say it has helped thousands change their lives.

THE BEGINNING

My husband and I began our life together in love and struggling as college students. I always assumed that once my husband graduated from college, our financial life would turn around. Graduation came and went but life also changed. We purchased our first new vehicle and bought our first home, and our first baby arrived. All of these life changes contributed to our financial troubles.

Over those early years we fell into bad financial habits. We were not living extravagantly, but we were living beyond our means. We would run up our credit cards paying for groceries, diapers, and everyday life. The first time we maxed out our credit card we took out a home equity line to pay it off. This became a convenient, awful pattern. Back then the real estate market was strong, and every time we built some equity in our home, we'd refinance to pay off our newest credit card debt. We took money from everywhere we could. We paid off a vehicle not once or even twice, but three times because we kept borrowing money against it.

I just didn't get it. My husband was working three jobs and I was working nearly full-time while raising three children. I couldn't understand why we were never able to get ahead or even to make ends meet. Something had to change.

Then one day I decided that I had had enough of the frustration and stress. That's when I had a life-changing conversation with my uncle Richard. He was financially successful and I was hoping he could give me advice on how to turn our lives around. Uncle Richard invited my husband and me out to dinner to talk about our financial situation. I was all for it; however, my husband was very hesitant. He was embarrassed at our financial situation and didn't want anyone to know about our issues. But after considering the trouble we were in, he changed his mind. That night over sushi, we were taught the Five Lessons and we made the commitment that would change our lives.

Inspired by what we had learned, we decided to be wealthy. We began by starting a nest egg and making simple changes like cooking more meals at home and limiting the restaurants we ate at. I began thinking about every purchase. Was the purchase a need or a want? I learned that I had been spending money to fill an emotional void. How could I have missed that about myself? The amazing thing about living the Five Lessons was that I did not feel like I was missing out on anything in life. In fact, I was living a better life. Living the Five Lessons was bringing me and my family true happiness.

To build our nest egg, we began collecting silver coins. Instead of going out to lunch every day with coworkers, I would walk to a coin shop and purchase a piece of silver. (This helped my waistline as well as my nest egg.) Watching our nest egg grow was satisfying, and we involved our children in the excitement. To them our silver was like pirate treasure, and they would stack it up and count it. Soon they wanted to save too. This was just one of the many happy side effects I found in living the Five Lessons. Another benefit was that my marriage and my family relationships improved. We were working on goals together and communicating much better. My husband and I did not want to disappoint each other. If one of us fell or made a mistake, the other would provide encouragement to get us back on track. We were in this together.

The Five Lessons were powerful and motivating, and living them became almost an obsession for me. Some of my former weaknesses became strengths. I took my spending habits and turned them into saving habits. I got good at saving money. Being financially responsible brought independence. And it was fun. I was no longer dependent upon the credit card company or the bank. We had our first debt-free Christmas. Within just fifteen months we were completely out of debt with a nest egg of more than $30,000!

Now, almost a half decade after learning the Five Lessons,

we have created a new financial pattern that we hope will help us retire not just as millionaires, but as multimillionaires. Our life is full of opportunities and we're no longer focused on debt—instead we can focus on our family and living. The challenges of parenthood are enough without the worry and pain of debt. Life is good. My husband and I have traveled all over the world, we have nice things, and we've been able to help others.

Now it's your turn to learn from my uncle. I urge you to follow his advice, just as we did, and just as he did from his millionaire mentor. Am I grateful that I learned the Five Lessons?

What do you think?

WHY I WROTE A BOOK
ESPECIALLY FOR WOMEN

These are difficult times. Today most people aren't hoping for a yacht; they're praying for a lifeboat. Especially women. In today's economic climate the challenges women face financially have never been greater. That's why I've adapted the original *Five Lessons* book to specifically help women.

Truthfully, I never expected *The Five Lessons a Millionaire Taught Me About Life and Wealth* to become an international bestseller. As pleased as I was with the book's success, I was equally pleased to discover that women were especially receptive to its message. However, the more I interacted with women, in conferences and mentoring, the more apparent it became that I needed to adapt the Five Lessons in a way that would meet women's specific needs.

THE FIVE LESSONS IS ABOUT HOPE. HOPE FOR WOMEN. HOPE FOR FAMILIES.

Women have always had a varied and complex relationship with money. And it's getting more complicated. In the past few decades the relationship between women and money has become more entangled than at any other time in history. Love it or hate it, women and money are inseparable partners.

> *. . . the times they are a changin'.*
>
> —BOB DYLAN

WOMEN TAKE CHARGE

A recent Pew study found that married women claim to control the family purse strings two to one over their husbands, and are also more than twice as likely to have the final say on major household purchases. In fact, more than 80 percent of all consumer expenditures are made by women.

Women aren't just spending more, they're earning more. The number of women with six-figure incomes has quadrupled in the past decade. Among women with business degrees, 60 percent now outearn their husbands. This trend is likely to not only continue, but increase. Consider this fact: the average

American with a college degree earns approximately twice as much as a person without one. And at the current rate, by the end of this decade women will be receiving 50 percent more college degrees than men.

Women's influence with money extends much further than their homes. They now control more than half of all expenditures in corporate America. Currently, 38 percent of businesses are owned by women, contributing more than $3.6 trillion to the U.S. economy. Today, more than half of all new businesses in the United States are started by women, with all indications that this will continue well into the future.

A MAN IS NOT A FINANCIAL PLAN

—bumper sticker

Perhaps the most relevant of all financial trends for women is this: *more than 80 percent of all women (and their dependents) will be financially reliant on themselves at some point during their lives.*

Unfortunately, too many women are not prepared to deal with this reality. Outdated beliefs about money and women not only weaken women's ability to create their own financial success but actually endanger them and those they love.

The Five Lessons contained in this book, if followed, will lead to wealth and financial independence. I know. They've worked in my life. And they've worked in the lives of thousands of women I've counseled over the past twenty years. But more important than material wealth, these Five Lessons offer freedom in a world increasingly intent on creating financial slavery. *The Five Lessons a Millionaire Taught Me for Women* is more than a book—it's the first step in a revolution aimed at freeing women: helping them take back their lives, their homes, and their liberty. I invite you to join our movement.

The gifted millionaire who taught me these principles did so as an act of kindness and generosity. I am pleased to follow in his footsteps. I dedicate this book to all the wonderful women in my life.

—Richard Paul Evans

The Five

Lessons

a Millionaire

Taught Me

for Women

Hard Times

When I was twelve years old, my father, a building contractor, fell through a stairwell on a construction site and shattered the bones in both of his legs. My father was our family's only source of income. So when the accident left him with no income, massive medical bills, and no disability or medical insurance, the financial result was devastating. I come from a family of eight children, and money had always been tight, but now as my father lay in bed unable to work for nearly a year, we were in real trouble. We were forced to sell our home and move into a three-bedroom duplex. I slept on the floor outside the kitchen for two years. It was a time of fear. Mostly I was afraid of what would happen to my parents. I was afraid (irrationally) that my father would go to jail for not paying his bills. I remember a man standing at the doorstep yelling at my mother because we were late on rent. I also remember the embarrassment of telling a friend that he couldn't call me because our phone had been turned off.

The Chinese have a saying: *When the student is ready the*

teacher will appear. This is what happened to me. During this difficult time, a man in our area, a multimillionaire named Kerry Heinz, invited the youth to a free lecture at the neighborhood church. He wanted to teach us about money.

We were confident that he knew something about the subject. He owned the number one basketball team in America, drove an expensive car, and owned real estate and businesses all over the West.

He was also completely self-made. He came from Ashton, Idaho, a tiny farm town with only two thousand residents— "if," he told us, "you count the dogs and chickens." He was born during the Great Depression, and like so many others during that time, his family was destitute. They rented two rooms in the back of someone else's house. They had no running water, and in the freezing northern Idaho climate, the only heat source was the small stove they cooked with. He learned to work as soon as he could walk, digging up potatoes on local farms alongside the migrant workers. He had come a long way since then. He was now the wealthiest man I knew.

IS MONEY EVIL?

The first thing Kerry Heinz did that day was to pull a hundred-dollar bill from his wallet and hold it up in front of us. I stared in wonder. I had never seen one before. He asked, "Is money evil?"

Even though it was an evil we all wanted, we all quickly agreed that it was. We were, after all, in a church.

"The Bible," said a teenage girl piously, "says that money is the root of all evil."

Our mentor smiled. "You are referring to the New Testament scripture in 1 Timothy, chapter 6, verse 10," he replied. "And it does not say that. It says that the *love* of money is the root of all evil. There's a big difference. In fact, just one chapter earlier in Timothy, the apostle Paul says that if 'any provide not for his own, he hath denied the faith, and is worse than an infidel.' How can you provide for your own without money?

"How about the parable of the Good Samaritan? Jesus told us to be like the Good Samaritan, yet how many of you here today could afford to pay for a stranger's hospital treatment and housing for a week? The Samaritan was able to help because he had the financial means to do so. Without it he could only have offered minor assistance." He continued. "This church we're sitting in right now, where did it come from?"

We didn't know. Churches just kind of grew.

"This church was built through the generous contributions of others." He looked us over. "For many, religion seems paradoxical on the subject of wealth. On the one hand, it seems to tell us that money is evil. On the other hand, God often blesses the righteous with wealth and material prosperity. For instance, in the Old Testament, after Job endured his many trials and proved his devotion to God, he was given back twice his wealth and possessions. So was God rewarding Job's righteousness with evil? Of course not."

Our teacher's tone became more serious. "Like most things, money can be used for good or evil. Every week I see people in our area being helped through the generosity and financial ability of others.

"At your age, you have no idea how much money is spent on your behalf—oftentimes by people you will never meet and never thank. The day will come when you must make a decision: Will you be one who helps others—or one who looks to others for help? It's your choice. You can be part of the problem or part of the solution. If you want to be the latter, then listen carefully, because what I have to tell you today will change your life."

Fear is a great motivator, and I was afraid. I listened very carefully and took notes. The lessons he taught that day lit a flame of hope within me. For the first time, I believed that there might be more to life than the seemingly endless financial desperation that had been my family's lot. I thought about his words constantly and began living the principles he shared. I immediately saw a difference in my life, and that made my belief burn still brighter. By the age of sixteen, I had become somewhat financially independent. I bought my own clothes and my own car, and paid for my own entertainment. By eighteen, I had saved enough to finance college and a church mission. By the age of twenty-six, I had saved enough to put 25 percent down on a house on a beautiful tree-lined street. By the age of thirty-one, I had paid off my home.

Less than twenty years from the time my millionaire friend gave that talk, I returned to him with several million dollars I wanted his help in investing. He smiled when he saw me. "I understand that you've done all right for yourself."

"I have you to thank," I said. "You taught me what it takes to succeed financially."

"You have yourself to thank," he replied. Then his smile turned to a look of concern. "I'm afraid you were the only one who listened to me that day."

"Maybe I was just the only one who thought he had to."

THE MILLIONAIRE IN YOUR MIRROR

Why is it that wealth seems so distant from most people? A while back my ten-year-old daughter asked my wife, Keri, if she'd ever seen a millionaire.

> KERI: (Smiling) As a matter of fact, I saw one this morning.
> ABIGAIL: (Amazed) Really? Was he wearing a crown?
> KERI: No.

ABIGAIL: Was he in a limousine?

KERI: No, he was just walking.

ABIGAIL: (Thinking about this) Were people dancing around him saying, "Go millionaire, go millionaire"?

Millionaires are not as removed as you might think. There are more than 3.5 million of them in the United States alone. In fact, even without a college degree the average American will earn more than a million dollars in his or her lifetime. So will you someday be a millionaire? According to financial trends, it's not likely.

Recent statistics given by the Federal Reserve indicate that household debt is at a record high relative to disposable income. In 1946, household debt was 22 percent of personal disposable income. Today it's more than 130 percent. And what about savings? It's hard to believe that at one time this country had an average savings rate above 26 percent. From 1948 to 1992 we averaged 7 percent to 11 percent. By the end of 2007 the U.S. savings rate became nearly nonexistent at an appaling 0.4 percent, the lowest rate since the Great Depression. Not surprisingly, personal bankruptcies in America have more than doubled in the past decade. In fact, far more Americans declare bankruptcy each year than graduate from college.

What about our retirement? If we take one hundred Americans and follow their financial path to age sixty-five, fewer than four will have an income above $35,000, while five times that number will live below the poverty line. More than 50 percent will be wholly dependent on relatives, Social Security, and welfare.

Now consider how women fare in retirement. First, they're mostly alone. Between the ages of seventy-five and eighty-four only a third of women are married with a spouse present. By the age of eighty-five that number drops to just 13 percent. Women, on the average, live longer than men and need more money saved for retirement—but they don't have it. In 2004, the median income for retired women was only $12,080, compared with men's $21,020.

If Americans' individual financial prospects seem so dire, then who and where are these millions of millionaires? What is it that makes these people wealthy and others not?

IS IT LUCK?

"Fickle fate" is a vicious Goddess who brings no permanent good to anyone. On the contrary, she brings ruin to almost every man upon whom she showers unearned gold. She makes wanton spenders who soon dissipate all they receive and are left beset by overwhelming appetites and desires they have not the ability to gratify.

—GEORGE S. CLASON, *The Richest Man in Babylon*

It's disturbing to me that a recent poll revealed that a large number of Americans think the best way to become wealthy is by winning the lottery. Let me put this in perspective: the National Safety Council accident tables show that in a single year, you're thirty times more likely to be killed by lightning than win the lottery. You're also more likely to die by poison, a rattlesnake bite, legal execution, or to be struck dead by a car.

Wealth is far more than just luck. Only 2 percent of today's millionaires inherited all or any part of their homes or property. Fewer than 20 percent inherited even a small portion of their wealth. And those "lottery winners" don't often retain their prizes. One study showed that of those who came into fortunes through lotteries, more than 80 percent were bankrupt within five years.

I was speaking in Cincinnati when a woman in the audience raised her hand. "I know exactly what you mean," she said. "I had the best job in the world. I was the nanny for the winner of the Florida Lottery. It was amazing. We traveled, ate at the best restaurants, had amazing parties, and they'd buy a new car every month. It was great while it lasted. Today they're bankrupt and live in a mobile home to flee their creditors."

This story's ending is the norm, not the exception. The fate of those receiving other windfalls, such as insurance claims, legal settlements, and inheritance, isn't much better.

IS IT INTELLIGENCE?

If wealth were simply a matter of intelligence, a disproportionate number of millionaires would have stellar IQs and academic merit badges. This is not the case. Most of today's millionaires did not graduate with high honors. Most of them did not even qualify for a top-rated college. In light of this, it is not surprising that Warren Buffett, the self-made multibillionaire investor, was rejected by Harvard Business School. In fact, research shows that millionaires' average grade point average is lower than a B.

On the other hand, highly academic, well-educated people often act like complete fools when it comes to personal finances. It is common knowledge among financial consultants that America's most educated citizens—doctors and lawyers—are notoriously bad at handling their money.

WHAT IS IT?

If it's not luck or superior intelligence that makes a millionaire, then what is the common denominator (besides money, of course) that the wealthy have and the rest of humanity does not? It's simply this:

The wealthy understand the principles of accumulating wealth and live them.

Some wealthy people learned the principles of accumulating riches through trial and error. Some—like myself—learned from mentors or parents. And for some, it just came naturally. But whatever this knowledge's source, I do not know a single self-made millionaire who does not understand and apply the five principles my millionaire friend taught us that day.

This is good news for everyone else. Because it means that wealth is less a matter of circumstance than a matter of knowledge and choice. Your knowledge of the Five Lessons means that you can choose to live the life you desire. So ultimately it comes back to you. Do you want to be wealthy? If so, let's get started.

LESSON ONE

Decide to Be Wealthy

WHO WANTS TO BE A MILLIONAIRE?

Women have been so brainwashed by the destructive female culture that taught them to associate money with sin, evil and everything crude, that it would take an entire book to disentangle the subconscious fears and incredible fantasies that the simple noun "money" evokes in most women.

—BETTY LEHAN HARRAGAN

I've seen it far too many times to deny it—the collective discomfort that falls over a crowd of women when I tell them to "decide to be wealthy." This shouldn't surprise anyone. The feelings women hold about money are remarkably complex and sometimes not even understood by the women who hold them.

Traditionally men and women have had different relationships with money. While women usually labor under society's crushing expectations of physical appearance, men's feelings of self-worth are more likely tied to their bank accounts. Men are not only encouraged to pursue wealth but pressured to do so. Women are usually taught the opposite.

This lack of female emphasis on money, combined with complex and often contradictory beliefs about wealth, leads to a general paralysis on the financial front. And those who fail to act, fail. As Lois Frankel wrote, "If you're like most women, you don't 'think' rich—and if you don't *think* rich, you certainly don't consciously engage in behaviors that will contribute to *getting* rich."

> I don't know much about being a millionaire but I'll bet
> I'd be darling at it.
>
> —DOROTHY PARKER

Even today, women are still more likely than men to be taught that their roles have less to do with money than with relationships. I, for one, applaud this teaching—*for men as well as women*. Life isn't about money. It's about God. It's about love. It's about family and relationships. It's about personal evolution, learning, and growth. And anyone who tells you otherwise is probably trying to sell you something. I can't think of any more sure method of creating an unhappy and unfulfilled life than to devote it to the primary pursuit of money.

However, the pursuit of financial power to secure and enhance life's true needs is not only appropriate, but wise. For those who do not accept responsibility for financial matters, life is thrown out of balance. As a dentist friend once told me: "Those who don't think about their teeth are those who later in life spend the most time thinking about them." It's no different with money. It's not surprising, then, that the people I know who are the most obsessed with money are not the millionaires or even the billionaires. Rather, they are oftentimes the ones who are living paycheck to paycheck. To the financially enslaved, life becomes all about money. It's not.

In order to be truly happy, we must live balanced lives. To be in great fiscal health is very much like being in great physical health: it allows you to do more and be more, and it permits you to live your life free of constant pain and bondage.

LIFE'S BUFFET: A FABLE

A woman was looking for a place to eat when she spotted a sign outside a restaurant.

ALL-YOU-CAN-EAT SPECIAL. ONE DOLLAR.

She decided to give the restaurant a try. Once inside, she found another sign that read:

SEAT YOURSELF

The woman found a small table in a crowded corner of the restaurant and sat down. Soon a waitress greeted her. "What can I get for you?"

"I'll have the special."

"The special?"

"Yes," the woman replied, looking around. "What everyone else is having."

The waitress handed the woman a plate. "Help yourself."

There was a long line at the buffet table, and when the woman finally got to the food she was disappointed by what she saw. Most of the bins were empty or appeared to have been well picked over. What was left didn't look very appetizing. *No wonder it's only a dollar*, she thought. She took what looked palatable and then went back to her table dissatisfied with her meal. When she had finished eating she went to the checkout counter to pay.

As she pulled out her wallet she noticed another room in the restaurant. It was much nicer than where she had dined and there were fewer people. There were chandeliers and beautiful carpets. The tables were covered with clean white cloths and set with china and silverware. There were long buffet tables laden with food: shellfish and roasts, colorful vegetables, and large platters of cakes, chocolate truffles, and desserts of all kinds. A chef stood at one end slicing great slabs of roast beef with a carving knife.

As she paid for her meal the woman asked the waitress, "How much is that buffet?"

"One dollar," the waitress replied.

"One dollar?"

She nodded. "Everything here is the same price."

"What? How come you didn't tell me about that room?"

The waitress looked at her with a perplexed expression. "You said you wanted what everyone else was having."

This little tale demonstrates *precisely* how most people live their lives. Why wouldn't you decide to be wealthy?

Money is a powerful ally. With money I've been able to provide life's necessities for my family and loved ones: food and comfortable shelter, as well as superior education and medical care. I have a child with special medical needs. A few summers ago our out-of-pocket medical expenses totaled more than $50,000. At that difficult, difficult time I was grateful to be able to care for my child without worrying about the money.

I think the best example of the power of money comes from an experience with my mother. A few years back I went to visit my mother only to find her quite upset.

"What's wrong?" I asked.

"We can't keep up with the bills," she said. "We're going to lose our home."

"You're not going to lose your home," I replied.

"How can you say that? We've lost three homes before." (This was true.)

"You didn't have a millionaire son back then," I said. "I'll pay off your home right now. Who holds your mortgage?" (Isn't this a cool thing to be able to say to your mother?)

"No," my mother replied. "We're going to lose it."

It took me a moment to understand my mother's response. Then I realized that her previous experiences of losing homes had been so traumatic that her fear now outweighed reason. So I dropped the subject and took my mom out to get some pie. On the way home, we stopped at a bank and opened a special checking account. It was special for two reasons. First, it never emptied. I put $20,000 into the account and asked my mother to call me when it was getting low and I'd fill it up again. Second, no one could get into the account except my mother. It was important to her that no one else could threaten her security.

A week later one of my brothers asked if I had seen Mom recently.

"Sure," I said, "we had pie last week."

"She looks younger," he said. "I think they've changed her medications."

*   *   *

I lost my mother several years ago. The evening of her funeral my father came to me and handed me her checkbook. "This is yours," he said. "I think there's still money in it."

As I looked inside the checkbook I found, in her own handwriting, a list of my mother's simple pleasures. Bookstores, craft shops, her hairstylist—small things my mother loved. I couldn't have known that my mother would die so young. How grateful I was to be able to provide her with some joy in her last days.

With money, my wife and I have been able to build Christmas Box House emergency shelters to help abused and neglected children. Since we began, our shelters have served more than twenty thousand children. Wealth has brought freedom of choice and opportunity.

You can't tell me that money is evil. But I can prove to you that the lack of money is.

> **Lack of money is the root of all evil.**
> —George Bernard Shaw

Financial distress is evil. The American Bar Association has estimated that nearly 90 percent of all divorces over the past decade can be traced to quarrels and accusations over money.

Debt and poverty contribute to other serious social issues as well. Studies by the Child Welfare League of America have demonstrated a direct correlation between financial problems and domestic abuse.

And there's more bad news for the fiscally challenged. Numerous studies have shown a direct correlation between debt and health problems. One study published in the *Journal of Law, Medicine & Ethics* found that "nearly half the debtors reported that debt troubles had affected their health."

A few years back, the president of the American Medical Association told me about some interesting research. "If you take two people," he said, "with the same physical ailment and put them in the same hospital room, using the same doctor, the same medication, and the same treatment—the one with debt is twice as likely to die."

Debt creates hopelessness. And without hope we lose the will to live.

> Like everything else, money is either holy or unholy, depending on the purposes ascribed to it by the mind.
> —MARIANNE WILLIAMSON

I'M NOT WORTHY!

One of the most perplexing responses I hear from women explaining why they haven't developed wealth is that they feel undeserving of it. I've heard this many times: "I don't feel worthy to be wealthy."

What does worthiness have to do with being wealthy? Would you say, "I don't feel worthy to be healthy?" Of course not. That would be silly.

Men don't generally have this problem. Not because they have higher self-esteem than women, but because they have never been taught that money is something you have to be worthy of. Unfortunately, the opposite is more true; many men feel that if they don't have a high net worth they aren't worthy. The truth is, neither attitude is correct or empowering.

The bottom line is this: money is power. And power in the hands of good people is a very good thing.

> **To deny we need and want power is to deny that we hope to be effective.**
>
> —LIZ SMITH

In the end, each person's definition of wealth is personal. For me, when a person no longer has to think about money, then they are truly wealthy.

The good news is that, for the most part, the decision whether or not to become wealthy is ultimately yours. As my millionaire mentor said, "You can either become part of the problem or part of the solution." My life changed the day he taught me this principle, because that was the day I decided to be wealthy.

EXTRAVAGANT≠WEALTHY

The most substantial people are the most frugal and make the least show, and live at the least expense.

—FRANCES MOORE

Before you can make the decision to be wealthy, you must have a concept of what being wealthy looks like. Understanding wealth begins by discarding the distorted, media-engendered notions you may have acquired concerning what it means to be rich. America's wealthy are too often stereotyped as having gaudy, extravagant lifestyles and irresponsible fiscal habits. The media perpetuates this caricature by focusing on the small percentage of wealthy individuals who live such lives: Lifestyles of the Rich and **Stupid**. While such people do exist, they are the exception, not the rule.

Two groundbreaking books have done much to shed light on the reality of America's millionaires. *The Millionaire Next Door,* by Thomas J. Stanley, PhD, and William D. Danko, PhD, and Stanley's *The Millionaire Mind* reveal that today's millionaires are remarkably frugal with their money. In fact, in many cases, even their own children do not know of their wealth.

Living lives of excess, exorbitance, and waste are counter to the message of this book. And, as I'll demonstrate later, such overindulgence is usually short-lived.

Most people you see trying to look wealthy are part of the look-rich-quick crowd. An expensive car or home does not make one wealthy. In fact, the opposite is more likely true. The path I'm recommending teaches individuals how to achieve a real and enduring affluent lifestyle based on spiritual and life-centered values.

THE POWER OF COMMITMENT

> It's a sad day when you find out that it's not accident or time or fortune, but just yourself that kept things from you.
>
> —LILLIAN HELLMAN

As simple as the First Lesson seems, in my experience it is the primary reason most women fail to achieve wealth—they simply never decide to be wealthy. They may hope or wish it to be so, but they never really choose it. The simple truth is, if you never choose to be wealthy, you will never attain wealth. And even if you do beat all odds and win the lottery, your wealth will likely be short-lived.

Choice is the beginning of all journeys. And, as with all first steps, it is the most important step of all. As Napoleon Hill wrote in his classic book *Think and Grow Rich:*

Riches begin with a state of mind, with definiteness of purpose, with little or no hard work.

There is something very powerful about commitment. Commitment to a plan or thought carries with it a remarkable force that influences the unconscious mind and brings about the desired effect. In other words, once we decide to have something, the mind unconsciously begins to create the reality necessary to bring to pass the very thing we desire. The opposite is true as well. If we believe that we can't do something, we can't. If we think we will fail, we probably will.

ASK AND YOU WILL RECEIVE

In recent years there's been a lot of talk about the "law of attraction." I don't disagree with this principle. I've always believed that the power of desire has great spiritual implications. As the Bible says, "Ask and you shall receive."

About twenty years ago I had the desire to travel to China. I didn't have sufficient funds at the time to justify such an expensive trip, but I wrote my desire down on a list of goals for the year. Four months later, a friend called me out of the blue. She had just won an all-expenses-paid trip to China for two. Her husband didn't really want to go, so she asked if my wife and I would like to take the trip instead. Of course you could call that a coincidence, but the odds of something like that happening would suggest otherwise.

TO CHOOSE THE PATH IS TO CHOOSE THE DESTINATION

There is a Chinese saying: *The journey of ten thousand miles begins with one step.* It's within your power, right now, to take the first step to wealth. Just one small step. Decide to be wealthy. Declare your intention by saying it out loud, then write on a card:

Today I decide to be wealthy.

Now put that card on your nightstand or next to your toothbrush. Read those words every morning when you get up and every evening when you go to bed. Keep a copy of it in your wallet next to your credit card. Do this for the next thirty days.

While it might seem a little peculiar writing down your intention, do it anyway. Psychologists have proven that the simple act of writing down an intention—even if you don't fully believe it—can yield powerful psychological results. And remember, the acquisition of money is, above all, a psychological process.

Now congratulate yourself. You have just taken your first step on a remarkable journey.

A wise Five Lessons disciple told me that she had written
TODAY I DECIDE TO BE WEALTHY
on more than a dozen cards and taped them all over her house.

"What should I do?" she asked. "My husband keeps teasing me about the cards."

"Did he ask you to take them down?" I asked.

"Heavens no, he loves the idea. He just likes to tease me."

LESSON ONE

Decide to Be Wealthy

LESSON TWO

Take Responsibility for Your Money

Rose, an intelligent, educated woman, grew up in a home where money wasn't discussed. Her father provided a good income for the family, and Rose and her siblings just assumed that money "grew on trees." Shortly after she was engaged to be married, she was surprised when her fiancé wanted to talk about finances. That's when Rose showed him her Magic Bill Drawer. Instead of paying bills she simply took the unopened envelopes and dropped them into a drawer where she hoped they would just magically disappear.

Far too many women are like Rose. While research suggests that more women than men are controlling the purse strings, too many women are still in a haze when it comes to their complete financial outlook. And if you don't control your money, your money will control you.

Taking control of your money begins with taking responsibility for it. That means knowing four things: how much you have, where it's coming from, where it's going, and what it's doing to make you rich.

Taking responsibility for your money also means not completely turning it over to a bookkeeper or spouse. It's a matter of personal stewardship. It's like parenting: you cannot leave the responsibility of your children to someone else and just hope that they'll turn out all right.

Of course, it's not just women who fall prey to fiscal irresponsibility. Men are equally fallible. A high-incomed friend of mine, finding his bank account depleted after burning through tens of thousands of dollars, said to me, "We have nothing to show for it. All I can figure is that we spent all our money on Happy Meals."

"Happy Meals?" I repeated.

"Yeah, the only thing different in our lives is a giant tub of Happy Meal toys."

Unfortunately, most women's closets are more organized than their finances. If you're one of the fiscally irresponsible, it's time for change. Taking control of your money begins with taking responsibility for it. You're good at taking responsibility for so many other things in your life; money should be one of them.

A NEW BEGINNING. A NEW LIFE.

The secret of getting ahead is getting started.

—SALLY BERGER

No matter how irresponsible you've been in the past, or still are, it's never too late to take control. Here are four steps to assist you in taking responsibility for your money.

1. KNOW HOW MUCH MONEY YOU HAVE

How much are you really worth? I was standing before a thousand women when I asked how many of them could tell me, within a few thousand dollars, their current net worth. To my dismay, only three in the audience raised their hands. I can't overly stress the importance of a woman fully understanding her net worth. Remember the statistic I shared at the beginning of this book: more than 80 percent of all women will be financially dependent upon themselves sometime during their lives. With odds like that, knowing your financial situation isn't just smart, it's vital.

Net Worth and Men

A woman said to me, "I can't ask my husband where the money goes or he'll think I don't trust him."

Unfortunately, she's not alone in her plight. A recent study showed that a large percentage of marital fights about money focus on financial control. We all know that women and men see things differently. A study showed that a man who doesn't share financial information is usually seen by women as controlling and power hungry. The same man may just see women as untrusting. Recognizing the reality of these contrasting viewpoints can help you achieve your goal without causing hurt feelings and conflict. Point out to your spouse that knowing your financial situation is not only in the greater good of your relationship and your family but also vital for self-preservation.

Nearly every time I speak on the Five Lessons, I hear the same heartbreaking story from some woman who was financially in the dark when her spouse died or divorced her. Only then did she learn of their dire financial situation. One young widow told me that her now deceased husband had run up debts of more than $200,000 that she didn't know about. Now she needed to somehow repay that money while taking care of her children—all on her own.

Perhaps a conversation along these lines may be beneficial:

JILL: Thank you for doing so much to make sure our family is financially taken care of. I don't know what we'd do without you. But I do worry about what we *would* do if something happened to you.

JACK: (Feeling praised and important) Nothing is going to happen to me.

JILL: I sure hope not. Of course, no one knows what will happen in the future. But I do know that you would never want to leave our family's survival to chance.

Roles

A woman I met on a flight told me that she believes men are meant to be the head of the household and that means she should trust financial affairs to her husband.

Even if this is your belief, being informed does not mean you are not trusting nor that you are taking control. It means that you are doing your share to protect your family and yourself. I can't imagine that any caring man would deny this necessity to his partner.

Show Me the Money

It wasn't until my husband and I divorced that I discovered that a third of our income had been feeding his gambling habits . . .

—SARA H.

You would be very concerned if you had a business partner who refused to show you the company books. This is no different in a marital partnership. As unromantic as it sounds, you *are* business partners. Unfortunately, a spouse who is excessively reticent in sharing financial information may be hiding something: debt, gambling, addictions, or other vices. If this is the case, the sooner you know the truth, the sooner you can help him and protect yourself. Remember, even if *he* creates the debt *you* are still responsible for it. On the brighter side, couples who work together on accumulating wealth usually enhance other areas of their marriage, as they develop greater trust in each other.

Know Your Net Worth

The Net Worth form in the Resources section of this book will help you calculate your current net worth and will give you a starting point for your wealth accumulation. Think of it as stepping on a scale at the beginning of a weight-loss plan.

At the end of each month, complete the report again to chart your progress. Then, at the end of each year, fill out an annual report. This will give you the most accurate view of your accumulating wealth. As your wealth grows, you'll find yourself looking forward to completing the forms.

2. Know Where Your Money Comes From

Every paycheck, bonus, interest payment, alimony check, child-support payment, royalty, dividend, gift, and tip you receive should be recorded on a ledger as income.

This will also help you understand your *real* income. I met a woman who wanted to be a stay-at-home mother but made the difficult decision to go to work to supplement an inadequate household income, only to find that they were worse off than before. She failed to take into account the added taxes, a higher tax bracket, child care, and other incidental expenditures, such as transportation to her job, a new wardrobe, and eating out. Knowing where your money comes from means an accurate portrayal of real income and the cost of that income.

Knowing where your money comes from will also help you decide how your money should be used. Ongoing income, such as your monthly salary and alimony or child-support payments, should cover ongoing expenditures. One-time money, such as a bonus or inheritance, should be used to pay for one-time expenditures, such as a vacation or an education fund, or for paying off debt.

3. KNOW WHERE YOUR MONEY IS GOING

While it is useful and important to know where your money comes from, understanding exactly where you are spending your money is the only way to gain control of it. You can't plug the holes in your boat if you don't know where they are.

You might have noticed (even been surprised) that I rarely use the word *budget* in this book. There's a reason for this.

Whenever you focus on deprivation you trigger the powerful "want instinct." (This is not to say that you should never deprive yourself of something.) The same is true for budgeting. When you try to force yourself to do something you don't want to do, you battle your greatest opponent—yourself. The best way to handle your excessive spending is to either lose the desire to spend or find something you want more. Like wealth, freedom, and security.

The first step in controlling your spending is to *identify* your spending. I recommend the use of a checkbook and a simple computer program such as Quicken. But technology is not necessary. For the first twenty years of my financial life, I kept track of my money in an inexpensive ledger I purchased at an office supply store.

In the Resources section at the end of this book is a Cash Flow form. This form will help you categorize all your income and expenses. You will notice that the first line under "Expenditures" is for documenting how much you are paying yourself. In the next chapter, Lesson Three, you will learn to always keep a portion of everything you earn.

The second expenditure on the form is for charitable donations. Lesson Five addresses this important item. The rest of your expense categories will depend on your chosen lifestyle. Each expenditure on your Cash Flow form represents an opportunity for reduction. To help you maximize your income,

I've compiled a tip sheet on ways to comfortably cut down on expenses in each spending category (see "Winning in the Margins with Savings" in the Resources section of this book).

More Than You Think

As you track your money, you will discover that most things cost more than you think. For instance, say you want to buy a larger home. If you're like most people you'll just look at how much extra your mortgage payment is per month. But the increased mortgage is just the beginning. There are the moving costs, Realtor commissions, and loan fees. There are extra property taxes, insurance, utilities, ongoing upkeep, and a thousand little extras from lightbulbs to furnace filters. If you have hired help, a larger home will cost more. If the home has a bigger yard there are also extra costs in landscaping, extra water, sprinkler repair, extra gas for the lawn mower . . . you get the idea. When you add up the real costs, what seemed like an acceptable increase suddenly doesn't look so attractive.

Learning where your money is going is the most important step toward gaining control of your finances. It is also an important way to gain control of your life. In the same way that knowing your net worth gives you control, so does tracking your money.

4. Know What Your Money Is Doing

Money makes a good servant but a bad master.

—French proverb

The world's wealthiest individuals and families make money by *managing* their money. The point of amassing wealth is to make money work *for* you instead of *against* you. Eventually, as you stay true to yourself and the Five Lessons, your money will earn more each year than your salary. Money will become your servant instead of the other way around. If you had an employee who sat around and did nothing, you would quickly fire her. Ongoing monthly evaluation of your investments is vital to your financial success. As you fill out your monthly Net Worth form, you will see clearly just how hard your money is working for you.

Knowing exactly where you should put your money to make it work for you is a more complex matter and is addressed more fully in the next lesson.

"I don't have time for this . . ."

Saying that you don't have time to watch your money is like saying that you don't have time to watch the traffic signals as you drive. You don't have time not to. You spend thousands of hours each year earning—why wouldn't you take a few hours a month to track where it goes?

LESSON TWO

Take Responsibility for Your Money

Keep a Portion of Everything You Earn

You can't touch this.

— MC HAMMER

We've all read stories about celebrities declaring bankruptcy or whining about their financial woes. From rock stars pawning their Grammys in order to pay delinquent tax bills to former professional boxers waiting on tables, the list of financial casualties grows annually.

The questions I ask myself are: Why didn't they just put some of what they had someplace safe? Why didn't they save the proceeds from just one album or, in the case of the boxer, just one title fight? If they had, they'd still be wealthy.

IT'S NOT JUST THE CELEBRITIES

Of course, celebrities aren't the only ones making bad financial choices. A financial adviser told me the tragic story of a client who had been seriously injured at work, losing a limb in an on-the-job accident. In compensation, he had received a $3 million insurance settlement—enough, if properly handled, to enable him to support his family indefinitely at a salary 500 percent higher than what they were earning before the accident.

Almost immediately after my friend created a financial plan for this couple, they began to change. Seduced by their sudden riches, they began taking a little here and there, buying things, recklessly loaning money to family and friends, launching unwise business ventures—the list of expenses grew as their account diminished. At a subsequent meeting with this couple, my friend noticed that the woman was wearing the largest diamond he had ever seen. "She deserves it," her husband said, "after all she's been through with my accident."

In spite of my friend's ongoing counsel and encouragement, week after week the couple withdrew funds until, less than three years later, they were completely broke and were both out looking for work.

The reason they and others in similar situations fail is because they do not understand the principles of wealth, especially the Third Lesson: a portion of all you earn is yours to keep.

"But all I earn is mine to keep," I often hear.

If that's true, then why do you have so little of it left? The truth is that you give your money to everyone but yourself.

You've heard it said before and it's true: "It's not what you earn; it's what you keep that makes you rich." The wealthy woman pays herself first.

"Pay yourself first" is a popular modern financial catch-phrase, but it has actually been around for decades. Back in the twenties, George S. Clason wrote:

"I found the road to wealth when I decided that a part of all I earned was mine to keep."

How much should you pay yourself? "That depends a good deal," as the Cheshire Cat said to Alice, "on where you want to get to." And how fast you want to get there. Obviously, the more you put away, the faster you'll achieve your goal. Research shows that most American millionaires save between 15 and 20 percent of their incomes.

I recommend that you push yourself as hard as possible at first—just to test your limits. Then, when you ease back, you will find your comfort zone. However, the amount you save should be a minimum of 10 percent of your ongoing salary and 75 to 100 percent of your side earnings.

THE GOOD NEWS FOR WOMEN

Most research shows that women value savings more than men. One study, by Allianz, showed that women preferred financial security fifteen times more than financial status. That doesn't mean they always save, and many don't, but it does give women a psychological advantage.

One reader told me how her mother would stash away money in her stocking drawer. "It got us through some tough times," she recalled. Another woman told me that for years she had worked for a charity earning only a small wage. Unbeknownst to her husband, she had put away all of her earnings into a savings account. When her husband lost his job, they used her savings to live on until he found another job. Her advice to women: "Every woman should have her own secret savings account."

THE POWER OF COMPOUND INTEREST

Albert Einstein is believed to have called compound interest "the greatest mathematical discovery of all time." Too many women either do not realize the power of compounding interest or simply do not take advantage of it. The following tables illustrate the power of compound interest.

In 2007 the median American household income was $50,233 a year. If Ms. Average allocates 10 (or 15 or 20) percent of her income to her nest egg and earns an average interest rate of 10.2 percent* she will accumulate wealth at the following rates:

10%		15%		20%	
Year	Savings	Year	Savings	Year	Savings
1	$5,309	1	$7,964	1	$10,046
5	$32,862	5	$49,297	5	$65,725
10	$87,470	10	$131,215	10	$174,941
15	$178,213	15	$267,338	15	$356,427
20	$329,001	20	$493,535	20	$658,003
30	$995,932	30	$1,493,997	30	$1,991,864
40	$2,837,504	40	$4,256,539	40	$5,675,009

And it gets even better. Lesson Four describes a method that allows you to more than double your monthly contributions.

---

* In today's economy 10.2 percent may seem unrealistically high, but this number is based on the average S&P 500 return over the past fifty years.

"I can't save that much . . ."

Initially, putting 10 percent of your income into your nest egg may require some faith. But it's worth the leap. Over and over I've heard those who try say: "We've never missed what we put away. Where did the extra money come from?"

This is my theory. I estimate that most people are wasting between 10 to 20 percent of their income. That is, that much of their income disappears without a trace. This being the case, I tell them the good news about their dilemma: they can easily save and invest that much of their income and not notice any negative change in their current lifestyle. In fact, as my niece Heather noted, most of those I've helped have actually experienced an improvement in their standard of living. As they adhere to the Five Lessons and put money away, they find themselves managing the remaining percentage of their income much better than before.

STARTING YOUR NEST EGG

Remember, becoming wealthy is as much a psychological and emotional exercise as a physical one. Anyone who has ever dieted knows that it's easier to stick to a diet when you see immediate progress in the mirror and on the scale. Likewise, the most powerful way to encourage new wealth-accumulating behavior is to see visible, tangible results. I found that the best way to do that is to create tangible wealth—to have something you can watch grow. In fiscal terms, this is called a nest egg:

a sum of money put aside for future expenses.

Personally, I prefer the dictionary's older, original definition of a nest egg:

A real or artificial egg that is put in a hen's nest to encourage it to continue laying after the other eggs have been removed.

This definition alludes to a powerful psychological need for anyone attempting to accumulate wealth: the provision of incentives in order to spur further productivity. I cannot overstate the importance of creating an abiding mental concept of your nest egg.

The accumulation of wealth is a satisfying thing.
> —KERRY HEINZ, my mentor

When I was fourteen years old, I decided to start building my wealth by collecting precious metals. I couldn't afford gold coins, but silver was selling for around three dollars an ounce—about two hours of work at my part-time job. I took one of my mom's canning jars and began filling it with one-ounce silver rounds. This method of wealth accumulation had several advantages. First, the fact that the rounds were not actual currency lessened my temptation (and ability) to spend them.

Second, I could actually see myself growing richer. As a poor boy, I found it satisfying to watch my wealth increase and, as nothing fuels success like success, the desire to watch the pile of silver grow helped motivate me to save more. The coins multiplied quickly, and soon I had filled several jars. Then I filled an entire wooden chest with silver. I felt like a pirate with a treasure chest. By the time I was eighteen, I had saved thousands of dollars.

As my niece Heather collected precious metals she discovered two additional advantages. First, perspective. She began to weigh the cost of an item against the price of silver. For example, she'd reason, "I could take my family out for dinner or I could make dinner and buy four more pieces of silver."

Second, purchasing the silver rounds satisfied Heather's urge to spend. Like so many others, she had discovered that she was a shopaholic—so spending her money on silver was like eating her cake and having it too.

PRECIOUS METALS? REALLY?

Does it need to be precious metals? Of course not. Collecting silver coins worked for me because to me they *felt* like wealth. And that helped me to succeed.

A few years back I was dropping my son off at preschool when his teacher stopped me.

"Mr. Evans," she said, "I don't mean to delay you, but I just wanted to thank you. I read your money book a few months back and now I'm out of debt for the first time in my life."

"Congratulations," I said. "Tell me about your nest egg."

She looked at me quizzically. "How did you know I had started a nest egg?"

"Because the Five Lessons don't work if you don't start one," I replied.

She hesitated. "I didn't collect gold or silver," she said, a little embarrassed. "I didn't know how to. So I just filled jars with dollar coins. I've got these jars all around my house."

Of course putting money in jars isn't considered a good financial investment, but psychologically it was a great one. I ran into this same woman a year later. "How's it going?" I asked.

She stuck two thumbs up. "Never been richer."

PURCHASING PRECIOUS METALS

As with all investments, there are pros and cons to purchasing precious metals. Starting your nest egg with precious metals is good for emotional and security reasons, but in the long run, it is not likely to pay out the interest you need for steady financial growth. In the past fifty years, the average annual return on precious metals has been around 4.5 percent—less than half the rate of return of the S&P 500. However, as we've witnessed lately, in times of economic crisis, precious metals act as a buffer against loss. For this reason, I recommend starting your nest egg with some metals; then, after you've established your nest egg, enlist the help of a professional financial adviser and expand to other forms of investments.

If you're on a limited income, I recommend purchasing silver. I began with .999 pure one-ounce silver rounds as opposed to coins or bullion. You'll pay a bit more for rounds, but they offer a better guarantee of authenticity, and you'll recover the extra money paid when you sell. Be careful not to buy special collector's coins (unless that's your intention and you are sufficiently knowledgable), as they likewise carry a special premium, which may not be recoverable when it comes time to sell.

The same is true if you're purchasing gold. For gold, .999 pure one-ounce coins (as well as other weights) are minted in the form of Canadian Maple Leafs, American Eagles, Chinese

Pandas, and South African Krugerrands. (Even though they all contain one ounce of gold, there is usually a slight difference in the cost.) These gold coins are quite beautiful, and the smaller coins make lovely pendants.

Both silver and gold are available at coin shops and precious metal dealers. Be sure to shop around before you purchase, as dealers update their prices at different times of the day. You can track hourly precious metal prices at the Five Lessons Web site at www.thefivelessons.com.

SEEK PROFESSIONAL ASSISTANCE

Ultimately, how and where you keep your nest egg is a decision you should base on your own current financial needs and the availability of trustworthy financial counsel.

As your investment builds, take the time to learn more about investing and investment opportunities. Diversity is important. As your nest egg grows, you may want to have a combination of securities, precious metals, and real estate. A 401(k) with an employer's match can be a very powerful tool in building wealth. Above all, avoid risky schemes and investments, no matter the supposed payoff. Just as you would consult a doctor before making any serious decisions regarding your health, consult an established, successful investment counselor before you make any major investment decision.

Note: In the Resources section of this book is a glossary of financial terms to help you understand some of these investment options.

THE GOLDEN GOOSE

As your nest egg grows, you will begin to feel the power that comes from having wealth. And you will notice things that are within your financial grasp that were not available to you before. With this newfound power you will be tempted to dip into the nest and steal a few eggs. Resist. You are likely familiar with the fable "The Goose That Laid the Golden Eggs." In this story, a poor country man discovers that one of his geese lays golden eggs—but only one a day. At first, he is happy with his new riches. But as his wealth grows, he becomes greedy and impatient. Finally, he decides to cut the goose open to get all the gold at once. Of course, in so doing he manages only to kill the goose and gets no more eggs.

BULIMIC MONEY PRACTICES

A more modern frame of reference is that many women's money habits resemble an eating disorder. They save their money only to suddenly purge it in reckless spending. Bulimic behavior will doom your nest egg. George S. Clason wrote appropriately about this habit: "Fool, you eat your children."

Remember, the primary purpose of developing your nest egg is not to spend it but to make it earn money for you—just as the wealthy do. With patience, your nest egg will earn more income than you can working full-time—but only if you leave it alone long enough to allow it to grow.

DEBT, DIET, AND OTHER FOUR-LETTER WORDS

Here are the five steps to freedom from debt.

1. Record All Your Debt on One Sheet (if Possible) So You Know Exactly What You're Facing.*

Better the devil you know than the devil you don't. Write down the company or person you owe, how old the invoice is, the invoice number, and the amount. Make sure you don't miss a single debt, as having unaccounted debt pop up later is demoralizing.

2. Contact (Preferably Call) Everyone You Owe Money and Ask if They Will Reduce Your Debt.

You'll be amazed at how much you can reduce using the seven golden words. (You'll learn this powerful technique in

---

* For a FREE Debt Attack form go to www.thefivelessons.com and click on DEBT.

the next chapter.) A company I know of did this and knocked out more than a third of their debt in just one week. They found that many of their creditors were willing to accept as little as 30 percent of the invoice if they would pay off the debt quickly. (This required them to shuffle their payment priorities a bit.) You will probably be surprised at how many of your creditors will be willing to work with you. Most companies are so used to people trying to "run out on them" that someone trying to honorably pay her debts is a treat.

3. Consolidate Your Remaining Debt with the Lowest Interest Rate Possible.

If you are struggling with significant debt, you might want to consult with a CCCS*—a consumer credit counseling service—to create a debt repayment plan. Today, many people carry the bulk of their consumer debt on their high-interest credit cards. If this is you, take the time to transfer your debt to a loan with a more reasonable interest rate.

4. Pay Down Your Debt.

A question I often get is, "Should I pay off my debt before I start building my nest egg?" The answer is . . . *it depends.*

In most cases, I recommend using 10 percent of your funds

---

* For a CCCS recommendation go to www.thefivelessons.com and click on DEBT.

for debt repayment and 10 percent for your wealth accumulation, even if you are losing a few percentage points in interest. I call this the 10/10 payoff. The reason for this is psychological. It is important, emotionally, for you to see the growth of your wealth. If you're not seeing your wealth increase, you will be less motivated and, ultimately, less likely to succeed.

I can best explain this principle by sharing a true story. I once had a friend who weighed more than 350 pounds. After years of struggling with his weight, he decided to do something about it once and for all. He put himself on a remarkably intense and painful diet. For ninety days all he could eat was a foul-smelling protein goop four times a day. He was miserable, but he stuck to it. After the first thirty days he had lost close to fifty pounds. Although this was a tremendous success, to him it didn't *feel* like one. He still weighed more than three hundred pounds. No one (outside those of us close to him) was congratulating him or telling him how good he looked. With all the pain he had endured and with no positive reinforcement to inspire him, he eventually quit. I'll never forget the day he said to me, "C'mon, Rick. Let's go get some pizza."

Whether you've fallen a hundred feet or fifty feet deep in a well, it's still dark and cold. If you're $100,000 in debt and manage, through great sacrifice and hard work, to pay off $50,000, life doesn't really seem all that different, as you're still deep in debt. However, if you were to pay off $25,000 and had $25,000 in an investment account earning interest, you would *feel* different. Success fuels success. Lack of success fuels nothing.

There are two other reasons for my philosophy. First, I've noticed that people develop what I'll call a *debt metabolism.* This is how one woman explained her debt metabolism.

"It seems we've always had fifty thousand dollars of debt. No more, no less. Then, when my mother died, we were left an inheritance of a little more than fifty thousand. The first thing we did was to pay off all our debt. But within six months we were right back to fifty thousand in debt. If we had put the money aside or gradually paid off the debt I think we could have changed our habits."

The second reason for simultaneously saving and paying off your debt is that it will help train you for your new lifestyle. Once your debt is paid off, just apply the extra 10 percent to your nest egg to accelerate your wealth accumulation.

When should you pay off your debt before starting a nest egg? When your interest rate is hopelessly high and you can't get it reduced. But even in this case, I would still start a nest egg with 1 percent of my income just to create the habit and belief.

5. Don't Create Any More Debt.

This might be the time to cut up some credit cards. In today's world it's not necessarily realistic to not have a credit card, but you can cut down on the number of cards you have,* lower their limits, or, if you're unable to control yourself, change to a debit card. One of the worst things that could happen after you have consolidated your debt is for you to create a new form of debt. If you suspect that you're a compulsive or binge spender, get help now. (See more about compulsive spending on page 98.)

LESSON THREE

Keep a Portion of Everything You Earn

---

* Note: closing a credit card account may affect your credit score.

Win in the Margins

Yesterday I dared to struggle. Today I dare to win.

—BERNADETTE DEVLIN

Of all the lessons, Lesson Four has the most to do with the speed of my own financial success. What does it mean to *win in the margins?* Simply this:

The wealthy find additional ways to add to their growing nest egg.

J. Paul Getty, once named the richest man in the world by *Fortune* magazine, called this "the Millionaire Mentality":

"The Millionaire Mentality watches costs and tries to reduce them—and strives to increase production and sales and thus profits."

Getty didn't write his 1965 book *How to Be Rich* for us "little people." He wrote his book for other business magnates. Lucky for us, we can still get a glimpse inside a billionaire's mind and learn some of his tricks.

There are essentially two ways to *win in the margins.* The first is by earning extra income. The second is by keeping more of what you earn. I recommend that you do both.

WINNING IN THE MARGINS WITH EXTRA INCOME

I once had a friend who had the peculiar habit of looking for money. He would actually walk or ride his bike while looking down. As odd as his behavior was, the most surprising result of his habit was that nearly every day he would find something. We would be walking along when suddenly he'd stop, bend over, and lift a coin or bill from the ground. I'm not recommending that you walk looking down. That's a little weird. My point in sharing this story is to demonstrate that you find what you are looking for. When you start looking for ways to increase your income, you will discover that there are opportunities all around you that you have never thought of or noticed. The following examples illustrate this principle.

COFFEE CANS OF GOLD

My wife's grandfather Pietro Disera emigrated from Italy to America when he was only seventeen. He came west looking for work and found employment in the gold and silver mines west of the Salt Lake Valley. He worked the night shift at the furnaces where the processed ore was smelted in order to separate the gold from the other metals before being poured into bullion. Pietro noticed that the molten gold would occasionally pop, splashing the metal on the hood of the furnace. He told his foreman that he would stay after his shift and clean the hood on his own time if he could keep the small metal flakes he found. The foreman agreed.

At the end of each shift, Pietro would climb into the furnace and scrape the thin gold flakes from the metal hood into an empty coffee can. Within months, the poor immigrant boy had filled two coffee cans to the brim with the precious metal—nearly twenty pounds of gold. That's nearly a quarter million dollars in today's money.

Stampin' Success

Shelli Gardner loved being a stay-at-home mom but yearned for a social and creative outlet. (And adding a little income to the family budget wouldn't hurt either.)

So Shelli and her husband took the money they were saving for a new home and started a rubber-stamp company called *Stampin' Up!* Shelli and her sister sold the stamps at home workshops and signed up family and friends to be demonstrators of their product, which includes rubber stamps and a wide variety of accessories. They stored inventory in Shelli's living room and filled orders while their children napped.

That didn't last long. Within months, the living room was far too small to handle the demand, and *Stampin' Up!* moved to larger facilities—twice in the first year. Two decades later, Shelli runs the international multimillion-dollar company, which has an 80,000-square-foot manufacturing facility and a 300,000-square-foot administration and distribution building.

Today, *Stampin' Up!* operates in seven countries with more than forty thousand demonstrators, and is helping other women to *win in the margins*. With such explosive growth, Shelli works hard to ensure that her original focus isn't lost. She believes that creativity, whether expressed in cards, scrapbooking, gifts, or home décor, can inspire others, strengthen relationships, and make people happier. It certainly has for her.

PROM QUEEN

Kathy Clifford was only eleven years old when she began designing dresses with her grandmother. Her passion for design carried on to college, where she majored in clothing and textiles. She met her husband there, married, and eventually had five children.

Kathy enjoyed life as a stay-at-home mother as she continued to design and make dresses for her three daughters. As her girls grew older, their friends also started asking Kathy to make their prom and pageant dresses. She often found herself sewing through the night to meet the demands of her unsolicited clients.

Then came the unexpected. Kathy's husband became seriously ill and was unable to work. The challenge of providing for five children suddenly fell on her. Though she had made money designing dresses, she couldn't sew fast enough to make the kind of money she needed to provide for her family, so she began researching how she could buy and market other dresses. One weekend she drove to Los Angeles and came home with twenty dresses. Now when people called to order a dress, Kathy explained that she couldn't sew a dress for them but asked if they would like to come over and see the beautiful dresses she had purchased. Her dresses were a hit and she purchased more. As her home filled up with dresses it became time to open a store.

At that time banks didn't particularly favor making loans to women. One bank manager told her that she'd be out of business in less than a year. But hearing "no" just increased her determination. Another challenge for Kathy was traveling around the world as a buyer without ever being taught how to do it. But, as Kathy says, "Women can do anything in the world that they want to do. There will always be someone willing to help them. And when there isn't someone, there's always a book."

Today, business at Kathleen's Bridal & Formal Wear is booming, and you can find her dresses advertised in *Seventeen, Your Prom,* and *Teen Prom* magazines. Kathy's dream has come true. She's a successful dress designer with buying power and clout, and enjoys seeing her designs create magic "on all the special days of a woman's life."

THE BOX

Randi Escobar and her husband, Tony, owned a nutritional products company that sold products to health food stores and pharmacies. When the tragedy of 9/11 hit, followed by the anthrax scare, they found it nearly impossible to import the materials they needed to produce their products. They were suddenly unable to fill orders, and their business collapsed. During this difficult time they clung together as a family and did what they could to get by. Randi still remembers just how much water you can add to milk before it doesn't taste like milk anymore.

Randi had been praying for something that would help her family recover from financial ruin when a cardboard box arrived on her doorstep. Her first thought as she picked it up was "Whatever it is, I hope there isn't a bill inside because I don't know how I could pay it."

Inside the box was a health product from Isagenix. It had been sent from an old friend with a note that read, "Please follow the instructions, use the product, and share with others."

Randi followed the instructions and had such wonderful results with the product that she signed up as a distributor with the company and began sharing it with everyone she knew. Within a few years, Randi had not only rescued their family business but, with her husband as her partner, went on to break network marketing industry records and become a multimillionaire. Today she is a global leader with the Isagenix company. But what she is most proud of is that twenty-six people in her team have also become millionaires and many more soon will be.

A Stupid Idea

As a child, Debbie Fields loved eating and baking chocolate chip cookies. She also enjoyed sharing her cookies with friends and family. While baking cookies might seem to be a simple thing, it was something she knew she was good at. In her teens she began experimenting with recipes and developing her own special one. She was only twenty years old when she had the idea to open a chocolate chip cookie store.

Debbie had married young, at the age of nineteen, and her husband told her the store "was a stupid idea." Her parents echoed the sentiment, telling her that without a college degree, business experience, or money, she had "no business going into the cookie business." Others just told her she was crazy. *How could a business survive selling just chocolate chip cookies?* But Debbie believed in her idea. And she wanted something more in her life. "It was about gaining control," she said. So without support from her family, she visited banks and investors. After being turned down again and again, she finally got a bank to loan her $25,000, and in 1977 she opened her first store in Palo Alto, California: *Mrs. Fields Chocolate Chippery.*

That humble store grew into a $500 million company with 650 retail bakeries in eleven different countries. Debbie became a business celebrity and inspired women entrepreneurs around the globe. She began franchising her stores in 1990, and sold the business to an investment group in the early 1990s. She has continued to innovate and has since authored several *New York Times* bestselling cookbooks. Debbie believes that "the biggest failure in life is never trying."

Of course, successful women's businesses are not limited to stereotypical female activities such as clothes, design, and cooking. Women can succeed in any realm of financial endeavor. In fact, two of *Women Entrepreneurs* greatest success stories are women in the petroleum business, their companies billing annually in excess of $100 million and $1 billion.

Undervaluing Your Abilities

One of the traits I often find women guilty of is *undervaluing their abilities and talents.* While it's common to find people with great talents who take their abilities for granted, women seem to be especially susceptible. "What I do is no big deal," they tell themselves. "Anyone can do it." The truth is, everyone can't. (Where would Debbie Fields be if she had thought, "Anyone can bake a cookie"?)

We're the same way about our ideas. All too often we discount them, storing them in the bargain bins of our minds just because they seem obvious or simple to us. In doing so we forget that the most brilliant of ideas are almost always simple in concept. Ralph Waldo Emerson said, "None of us will ever accomplish anything excellent or commanding except when [she] listens to this whisper which is heard by [her] alone."

Back when I was an advertising executive, our agency would focus-test products to learn how to sell them, or to discover if they were even salable. We'd fill a room with women, and then sit behind a two-way mirror and listen in as they discussed our product's benefits and faults.

I'm sure, if asked, those women would claim not to know anything about marketing, but the truth is, we were relying on them to tell us how to market. We valued and needed their input. *They* were teaching *us.* Bottom line: believe in yourself. Your opinions and ideas are far more valuable than you give them credit for.

SODA POP, TUXEDOS, AND CHRISTMAS GIFTS

The most money I've made in my lifetime was on a side project. It wasn't my first such venture. It was my fourteenth.

For me the habit of *winning in the margins* started when I was young. At the age of thirteen, I was working for low wages cleaning up construction sites. Such menial labor gave me ample time to think. (Though most of what I thought about was how I could quit cleaning construction sites.)

One afternoon I noticed that the welders (who were paid well) would leave the job site every few hours and drive to a nearby convenience store for soda pop. I saw an opportunity.

That night, on the way home from work, I bought an inexpensive cooler at a secondhand store, then purchased soda pop and candy bars in quantity from a nearby price club. The next day I took my cooler to work, selling my products at a dollar each. I doubled my income, making as much on the treats as I did pushing a broom.

I found another opportunity when I worked at a formal-wear shop. One day my boss asked me to carry some boxes up from the cellar. When I had completed the task I asked him what was in the boxes.

"Old suits," he replied.

I cut open a box and pulled out one of the suits. It was an old black tuxedo. It was from the sixties and looked like one of the Beatles' tuxedos. I asked him what he planned to do with the suits.

"I'm just going to haul them out to the landfill."

"Why don't we sell them?" I asked.

"Who would buy a twenty-year-old used tuxedo?"

"I would," I said. "May I try selling them?"

He rolled his eyes. "Sure. Just don't let it interfere with your work. And I'll tell you what. You can keep half of what you bring in."

The sale of those suits brought in more than $16,000.

My biggest success came ten years later when I decided to self-publish a book I had written as a Christmas present for my daughters. I hadn't intended to publish the book, but after receiving many requests for copies, I decided to print a few. The first year that little book netted me $20,000. I reinvested my earnings, and the second year I earned more than $400,000. The third year I earned nearly $4.5 million. That's when I quit my day job.

You could say that I—and the others I've written about here—were just lucky. Of course we were. But as George S. Clason wrote, "Opportunity is a haughty Goddess who wastes not her time with the unprepared."

Was it luck that caused me and my colleagues to try again and again to find ways to succeed financially? Was it luck that I noticed a trend with my book? Was it luck that I consulted all the experts I could find about making my book a success? Was it luck that I took copious notes on each marketing venture I tried, evaluating its successes and failures? The bottom line is (and you should underline this): I would never have been lucky had I not been looking for ways to increase my earning ability.

For free ideas on how to *win in the margins,* visit my Web site today at www.winninginthemargins.com and enter "win" when asked for your passkey.

DOUBLE YOUR WEALTH

While most of those in the previous examples hit it big, even earning just a percentage of your regular income each month goes a long way toward building your wealth. As indicated by the table showing compound interest in Lesson Three, if you're earning an average household income and are saving 10 percent, you are putting away about $418 a month. If you increase your income by an extra $418 a month and apply it to your nest egg, it is, in the long-term accumulation of wealth, the equivalent of doubling your income.

WEALTH ACCUMULATION AT 10 PERCENT:

Year	Savings
1	**$5,309**
5	**$32,862**
10	**$87,470**
15	**$178,213**
20	**$329,001**
30	**$995,932**
40	**$2,837,504**

WEALTH ACCUMULATION AFTER DOUBLING YOUR NEST EGG CONTRIBUTION:

Year	Savings
1	**$10,046**
5	**$65,725**
10	**$174,941**
15	**$356,427**
20	**$658,003**
30	**$1,991,864**
40	**$5,675,009**

By increasing its nest egg contribution through earning or saving an additional 10 percent each month, the average household will achieve millionaire status more than seven years earlier. Clearly the path of extra income is worth pursuing. But where do you find the extra income?

As demonstrated by my friend who walked with his head down looking for money, it's all around you. In the Resources section of this book, under Winning in the Margins with Extra Income, is a list of possible additional sources of income. However, your greatest success *winning in the margins* will likely come through paying attention to your talents, abilities, and the unique opportunities that already surround you.

I suggested earlier that there's another way to double your contribution to your nest egg that doesn't include extra earnings: saving. It's the second way to *win in the margins.*

WINNING IN THE MARGINS WITH SAVINGS

Money has wings.

—Proverbs 23:5

THE WORLD IS DESIGNED TO TAKE YOUR MONEY.

Successful wealth-building women understand that the world is designed to take their money. Never forget that. Billions of dollars have been spent to suggest to your mind what will make you happy, what you should look like, what you should drive, eat, and wear, and, ultimately, how you should spend your money.

The collective power of those suggestions is probably far stronger than you realize. Just look at a twenty-year-old fashion magazine. What were we thinking? Or was someone thinking for us?

Early in my advertising career, I wrote a radio commercial for a local chain of copy centers. In this commercial, I depicted a man talking about the copy centers' new, longer hours with a customer who showed up at his store at five minutes past five o'clock needing exactly three thousand copies by morning.

The radio spots ran, and to our surprise, the managers at each of the seven copy centers reported that they had had a rush of people showing up at 5:05 P.M. needing exactly three thousand copies by morning.

In the same way that the Millionaire Mentality recognizes that the world is designed to take our money, it also knows that the average American has been psychologically conditioned to consume and spend. Market researchers and retail anthropologists specifically study your shopping behavior to more efficiently target you. On the Internet, computers track your spending habits and systematically parade offers in front of you. Politicians and bureaucrats increase fees and taxes. Determined salespeople take courses to learn how to get you to part with your money.

And it's getting worse. Marketers are targeting younger and younger consumers, addicting them to a lifestyle of over-consumption. From 1980 to today, advertising to children in America has increased more than tenfold, from $100 million a year to more than $1 billion.

Successful wealth builders recognize the nature of the real world and therefore carefully scrutinize every expenditure. They learn to *win in the margins* by keeping more of what they earn.

While most of today's self-help books spout messages about thinking big, J. Paul Getty argued in *How to Be Rich* that the problem of financial failure is often attributable to the inability to think small.

The Millionaire Mentality, he wrote, "gives meticulous attention to even the smallest details and misses no opportunities to reduce costs in his own or his employer's business." We can change that to ". . . and misses no opportunity to reduce costs in her own business and household."

This Millionaire Mentality can be applied to all aspects of financial endeavor, from business to personal spending. There are four key mind-sets that characterize the effective wealth builder:

The Five Lessons a Millionaire Taught Me for Women

1. The Millionaire Mentality carefully considers each expenditure.
2. The Millionaire Mentality believes that freedom and power are better than momentary pleasure.
3. The Millionaire Mentality does not equate spending with happiness.
4. The Millionaire Mentality protects the nest egg.

I will examine each of these Millionaire Mentalities in greater detail.

The Millionaire Mentality Carefully Considers Each Expenditure

"Economy, prudence, and a simple life are the sure masters of need, and will often accomplish that which their opposites, with a fortune in hand, will fail to do."

—CLARA BARTON

There are three questions that the successful wealth builder asks herself before she parts with her money.

1. Is this expenditure really necessary?
2. Is this expenditure contributing to my wealth or taking from it?
3. Is this an impulse purchase or a planned purchase?

1. Is this expenditure really necessary? (Or is it possible to get the same personal effect without using money, or using less of it?)

One of the best-dressed women I know is a single mother living on a very limited income. "How can you afford such a beautiful wardrobe?" I asked her. She smiled and said it was her secret. Later on she offered to tell me. "I only buy used clothing—high quality—but preowned by some rich person. I let them lose the value." Same effect, without the financial effect.

A few years ago I was in Venice, standing near the gondolas by Piazza San Marco. I had lived in Italy for more than a year and spoke enough Italian to be conversant. The gondoliers, however, assumed that I was just another American tourist, so they didn't worry about what they said in front of me.

"How much do I charge this group?" one of the gondoliers asked.

"Fifty euro for Japanese. Forty euro for Americans. Twenty euro for Italians."

"How do you determine what to charge?" I asked the man in Italian.

Embarrassed that I had understood him, he finally answered, "Whatever they will pay."

More prices than you think are determined in this very way, and as such are usually far more negotiable than you think. This doesn't mean you have to become a hardened haggler. Simple, soft-voiced inquiry is often just as effective—if not more so. Recently I was shopping for some computer equipment at a local electronics dealer. After the salesperson had demonstrated the equipment and quoted a price, I simply asked him if they matched the lowest price available. "I hate buying something and the next day finding it cheaper somewhere else," I explained. He thought about it, then said, "Just a minute." He pulled up a comparison site on the Internet, and we immediately found the same equipment available for $140 less.

"There's the price," I said.

He not only sold it to me for the lower price, but he threw in a few other complimentary items as well. Many people don't get what they want out of life simply because they don't ask.

THE SEVEN GOLDEN WORDS

A salesman friend of mine was trying to negotiate a deal with a large client. When he quoted his bid, his client's forehead creased with concern. "Is that the best you can do?" he asked.

My friend began to squirm. He left the room and called his boss. "We've got to do better," he said. His boss gave him a better price. Newly confident with his bid, my friend sat back down with his client. "We can go three percent less."

The man still looked concerned. "Is *that* the best you can do?"

My friend, more certain that he was about to lose the account, went back to the phone. He again talked to his boss, who conceded one more percent discount. Afraid that it wasn't going to be enough, my friend threw in a portion of his own sales commission. Still, the client didn't seem impressed. "Is that *really* the best you can do?"

My friend sighed. "I'm sorry," he said, "but it is."

The man smiled. "Fine. I'll sign the order. I was just making sure that it really was your best offer."

Winning in the margins means pushing the limit to see just how low you can purchase—especially on the big-ticket items.

A financial consultant once said to me, "It drives me crazy the way people compartmentalize their money. They'll clip coupons to save thirty-five cents on a can of soup, then throw thousands away on a big purchase because they didn't bother to compare prices or even ask if they could get it for less."

Just seven simple words: IS THAT THE BEST YOU CAN DO? Of all the advice in this book, the Seven Golden Words are most likely to provide you the most immediate and surprising success.

A friend of mine who was in the middle of building a home claimed to have saved more than $25,000 by using the Seven

Golden Words. And, he added, the subcontractors all thought that he was especially smart and actually added free upgrades.

I've had several readers report saving more than a thousand dollars within a few hours of learning the Seven Golden Words. In fact, we hear these success stories regularly. Not that this surprises me. I have a large and growing collection of my own. The Seven Golden Words work. Not always, but enough of the time to make them worth your while.

A New Baby

Ashley recently adopted a baby girl. Besides the normal fees associated with the adoption agency and lawyers, the medical costs associated with the birth were well over $20,000. Having used the Seven Golden Words before, she decided to see if she could lower this medical expense as well. After reaching the hospital's Accounts Payable office, Ashley first thanked the hospital representative for the care they had given her baby and her baby's birth mother. She then quickly described the events surrounding her baby's birth and kindly asked if the outstanding balance was "the best they could do." After a few minutes on hold, the Accounts Payable representative returned, happily saying that the hospital was willing to reduce the bill by 80 percent if she would pay the bill in full within thirty days—a savings of $16,000.

A BEDROOM SET

Patricia had saved three long years to purchase a bedroom set. When she had finally saved enough she went to the furniture store to pick it out. She found the set of her dreams and wanted to purchase it immediately but, having read *The Five Lessons,* decided to sleep on her decision. As soon as she got home she realized that she hadn't used the Seven Golden Words. She called the salesperson and asked him if the $6,000 price tag was the best he could do. "No," he replied, "I can give you thirty percent off." It worked so well she tried it again and asked if *that* was the best he could do. "Well," he said, "let's make it an even two thousand dollars off and I'll pay the sales tax and delivery."

Using the Seven Golden Words, Patricia saved more in five minutes than she had in a whole year.

RUBY SLIPPERS

Lisa was a little hesitant about using the Seven Golden Words, but eventually decided to give them a try. "What did I have to lose?" she reasoned. She found her opportunity a few days later when her friend introduced her to a new shoe store.

Lisa had already selected several pairs when she came upon some expensive red patent leather pumps. In spite of the price, she added them to her purchases.

Lisa had noticed that one of the other customers in the store had used a ten-dollars-off coupon. Lisa said to the salesclerk, "I don't have a coupon, but can I still get the discount?"

"Sure," the woman said.

Lisa thanked the woman. After the salesclerk had rung up Lisa's shoes, Lisa looked at the price and said, "Is that the best you can do on this price?"

The lady looked at her for a moment, then reached into a drawer and pulled out a special coupon and scanned it. The price changed.

"There you are. That's an additional eighty dollars off your purchase," she said.

Lisa was almost speechless but managed to thank the woman again.

When Lisa got home she captured her savings by putting the eighty dollars she had saved in her nest egg.

As consumers we leave a lot more money on the table than we realize. A woman at one of my seminars was the day manager at a national chain clothing store. "It's corporate policy," she told us, "that any of our employees can discount up to thirty percent off any product at any time. All a customer needs to do is ask."

"How long have you worked for that store?" I asked.

"About five years."

"In all that time, how many customers have asked for a discount?"

She thought about it for a moment then replied, "Maybe three."

The Seven Golden Words are one of my favorite tricks in this book. I hear more success stories from this technique than any other. I personally have saved more than $100,000 using these words.

The Seven Golden Words don't require haggling. In fact, the more softly and kindly you use them the better they work. That's because this approach isn't confrontational, it's cooperative.

A few years back a man came up to me after one of my seminars. "Those Golden Words of yours don't work," he said bluntly.

"Really?" I asked. "You've tried them?"

"Well, not exactly. I got my own method."

"Tell me about it," I said.

"I look them in the eye and say, 'It ain't worth that.'"

"And?"

"In forty years it's never worked."

"Hmm," I said. "Think of it this way. If I'm at a book signing and you come up to me, pick up my book, look at the price, and say, 'It ain't worth that,' you've just offended me. In fact, I don't want you to have my book. However, imagine the opposite approach: you say, 'This book is worth twice this much. Unfortunately I can't even afford this price. Do you think that's the best the store can do?' What do you think I'm going to do? If I don't buy it for you myself, I'm definitely going to talk to a store manager to see if such a wise, kind man can get a much deserved discount."

He nodded but didn't get it. "To each his own," he said.

The Seven Golden Words are engaging. They are inviting people to be magnanimous and feel good about themselves. What I love most about the Seven Golden Words is that they are especially empowering for single mothers. Single mothers are constantly struggling with the balance of working more to provide for their families' needs or spending more time with their children. These women are heroes of mine. If a young single mother learns this one powerful technique, saves $100 a month using it, and puts it away in her nest egg, she'll retire with a fortune. Sure, retirement may seem a lifetime away, but wouldn't a $25,000 or $100,000 cushion in the bank change the way she views life?

JUST ONE THING

In junior high school I had a wrestling coach who said, "Evans, I don't care how many moves you know, I just want you to be better at one of them than anyone else in the state."

He told me a story about a wrestler who had practiced a take-down move every day until no one could stop him. He would take down his opponent, then just let him go and take him down again. He won first place in state every year.

Why am I telling you this story? If you can perfect just this one move, just seven simple words, then remember *to capture your savings,* you'll see remarkable success.

LESS IS MORE

As long as we're asking the question "Is this expenditure really necessary?" something should be said about consumption. Americans overconsume at record (and embarrassing) levels. The quest to have more can be seen in our homes as well as our waistlines. In 1950, the average home was 1,100 square feet. In 1970, it had increased to 1,400 square feet and by the year 2004, the average home was precisely 2,348 square feet, despite the fact that families have gotten smaller.

As a nation we are spending more and enjoying it less. Peculiarly, more people surveyed in the fifties described themselves as "rich" than do today.

Curtailing the pattern of overconsumption is an important step—not just in saving, but in freeing ourselves from our possessions. Psychologically, in spite of all we've been told (or sold), more is less and less is more. This is corroborated by a study that showed that 86 percent of Americans felt happier after having voluntarily cut back on consumption.

Now on to the second and third questions the successful wealth builder asks herself before she parts with her money.

2. Is this expenditure contributing to my wealth or taking from it?

Of course not all expenditures can be assets, but continually asking this question helps wealth builders redirect the use of their money. It's no coincidence that the wealthy put their money in their homes instead of their cars. Homes usually appreciate. Cars almost always depreciate.

3. Is this an impulse purchase or a planned purchase? Am I being pressured to make an expenditure I'm not certain about?

Candy bars and magazines line the checkout stands like thugs, waiting to jump you as you pull out your wallet or purse. Late-night infomercials come at you when you're tired and your resistance is down.

The impulse buy is the mainstay of the American retail establishment. The layout of the grocery store testifies to this, which is why the essentials—meat, eggs, and milk—are always at the back of the store, making you pass aisle after aisle of possible impulse purchases. And it works. Most grocery stores estimate that more than 50 percent of purchases are impulse purchases.

You've heard the adage "Never shop with an empty stomach." This wisdom should be applied whenever money is concerned. Never shop with an empty ego. Buy what you mean to buy. Whether it's for groceries or a new car, save time and money by shopping with a list.

GOING ONCE, GOING TWICE . . .

Early in our marriage, my wife and I made a commitment never to make any large purchase "on impulse." If the salesperson said he needed an answer "right now," then the answer was "no." In nearly twenty-five years, we haven't once regretted walking away from a strong-arm sales pitch. Not once. In fact, whenever we found ourselves being pressured by an aggressive salesperson—one who was insisting that we had to buy now or let a once-in-a-lifetime opportunity pass—it was very empowering to be able to say no.

The funny thing is that despite all the threats that the opportunity would pass, it never did. Not once that I can remember. But many times we passed. Often, after a good night's sleep, we decided we really could live without an automatic sock stacker after all.

Again, the Five Lessons are not about deprivation. They're about not wasting money. Buy whatever you want, if you have the money. Just make sure that you really want it and will enjoy it for at least as long as you have to pay for it.

CAPTURE YOUR SAVINGS

Everything you've just learned about saving is only half the process. Whenever you save money from using one of these techniques, it is important that you *capture those savings* by moving the money saved into your nest egg. For instance, a friend of mine was about to pay off a hospital bill and had already written out the check for $1,500 when he decided to try the Seven Golden Words. The hospital, apologetically, told him that it could discount the bill by only 10 percent. He was delighted, of course. He tore up the check he had written and wrote two more—one for the revised hospital bill of $1,350 and the second to his nest egg for the $150 he had just saved.

There's another psychological benefit to this technique. Have you ever trained an animal? The very foundation of successful training is to reward desired behavior. The same principle is true for humans. You're no animal, but whenever you save money *then capture those savings*, you are conditioning yourself for more success. The more you pay yourself and watch your nest egg grow, the stronger your habit will become.

Remember, if you are able to save just $100 a month and you faithfully transfer it to your nest egg, in forty years (compounded at the average S&P 500 rate of 10.2 percent) that little extra savings will be worth close to $700,000!

MIND-SET TWO

The Millionaire Mentality Believes That Freedom and Power Are Better Than Momentary Pleasure

> So many of us define ourselves by what we have, what we wear, what kind of homes we live in, and what kind of car we drive . . . If you think of yourself as the woman in the Cartier watch and the Hermès scarf, a house fire will destroy not only your possessions but yourself.
>
> —LINDA HENLEY

The sirens of credit are luring you to the rocks of disaster. Their enticing song, "Buy now, pay later," is indeed truth in advertising, though it was certainly not intended to be. *Pay* is exactly what America is doing. The price we pay to "have it now" is quite clear: broken marriages, homes, health, and lives. The successful wealth builder understands the danger of debt and knows that the primary way to avoid it is by delaying gratification.

A decade ago, *Time* magazine reported that brain research suggests that emotions, not IQ, may be the true measure of human intelligence. And the ability to delay gratification is one of the key indicators of emotional intelligence. Interestingly, it is also an indicator of future success.

THE MARSHMALLOW EXPERIMENT

A group of scientists created an experiment to test emotional intelligence. They told four-year-old children that they could have one marshmallow now or, if they could wait while the researchers ran an errand, they could have two. They then placed a marshmallow in front of each child and left the room. Some of the children waited for the second marshmallow, while others immediately devoured the one in front of them. The follow-up research was most fascinating.

Those children who could delay gratification "generally grew up to be better adjusted, more popular, adventurous, confident and dependable. Those who couldn't were more likely to be lonely, easily frustrated and stubborn. They buckled under stress and shied away from challenges."

In addition, those who could delay gratification also scored an average of 210 points higher on the SATs.

My Father's Epiphany

I'll never forget the night my father called us together for a special family meeting. It was after we had lost our house, and all of us children had gathered in the living room of our little duplex. The mood in our home that night was as somber as a funeral, and my father looked distraught. We didn't know why he had brought us together, but from his countenance, we knew it couldn't be good.

He said: "I've spent the last three days figuring out why, after all these years of hard work, I have nothing to show for it but bills. Do you know where it all goes?"

"To us?" one of us asked.

"No," he said grimly, "I wish it had. But it doesn't. It goes to interest. All those heartbeats went to paying interest to make someone else wealthy. Delay gratification. Never borrow money."

Earlier, in the Third Lesson, I demonstrated the power of compound interest. Never forget that compound interest is just as powerful working **against** you as it is working **for** you. What might seem like a small expense now can, in the long run, steal your wealth.

Simply put, there are two kinds of people: those who earn interest and those who pay it. That's the fundamental difference between the wealthy and the desperate. The Millionaire

Mentality sees clearly the danger of credit and knows that freedom and power are infinitely better than short-lived pleasure.

BUT I DESERVE IT . . .

An employee of mine desired a new car. It was too expensive for her income, but she was intent on convincing me that it was the right choice for her.

"My husband is about to get a raise. Why shouldn't I have a nice car? Don't I deserve it?"

Deserve it? She had just regurgitated the greatest marketing sham ever propagated on the American consumer—the result of years of advertising brainwashing. She deserves what? To find happiness based on something that will decay and lose value within a year, yet will continue to financially enslave her long after her infatuation with the metal is gone? In the words of my teenage daughter: Is this a good thing?

After several discussions, she reluctantly chose not to buy the car. A year later we revisited her decision.

"I'm so glad I didn't buy that car," she said. "It doesn't even interest me anymore. And my husband didn't get the raise we had planned on. Had we bought that car, we would have found ourselves deep in debt and struggling just to make payments."

The next time you hear someone say, "You deserve it," red flags should instantly go up in your mind. Someone is trying to take your wealth. Someone is trying to steal your dreams for themselves. What you really deserve is peace of mind, individual freedom, and personal power.

THE PAYDAY LOANS TRAP

Remember, it's them versus us. The payday loan industry is big business and getting bigger. In just eight years it's grown from $10 billion to $85 billion. And two-thirds of those funding this industry growth are women. *Women in financial trouble.* In fact, one payday lender's business plan unabashedly declares that "welfare-to-work mothers [are an] excellent opportunity for check cashing and cash advance businesses."

Sigh.

Predatory. Exploitative. Entrapment. These are just some of the terms used to describe this industry. That should be warning enough to stay away.

A payday loan is a short-term loan intended to "help" the borrower get by until the next payday. While there are laws regulating how much interest can be charged by financial institutions, these businesses get around these laws by charging "fees" rather than "interest." These fees typically account for 15 percent of the loan. If you do the math, you'll realize that if you continue to repeat (or roll over) the loan, your actual annual interest may be as high as 400 percent.

I've personally witnessed the damage using these loans can cause. An employee of mine had gotten behind on her bills and decided to get out of the bind by using a payday loan. Already short on cash, now, with 15 percent less cash a month, she was really in trouble. She found herself using cash advances more and more. One day she came to me in tears, embarrassed to tell me what she had done. "It was so short-sighted," she said. "It just seemed like a quick fix."

It was quick but not a fix. Eventually the "cure" became worse than the disease. Using payday loans can turn a temporary financial problem into a permanent one.

THE TRUTH OF THE PLASTIC

In 1968 credit card debt was $8 billion. Today, forty years later, that number has increased by more than a hundred times. With so much wealth at stake, it's no wonder banks and retail businesses work so hard to extend you credit. (There were 5.3 billion offers for new credit cards in 2007 alone.) And their efforts are paying off. In 1970, only 17 percent of American households had a bank-issued credit card. Today Americans own more than a billion credit cards. One in seven carry ten or more credit cards. I met a woman at one of my seminars who had twenty-seven different credit cards. When she ran out of money on one card she simply applied for another.

In addition to credit cards, there are other credit-inducing tactics you might not have considered. A common credit sales tactic is the no-pain add-on purchase. You've likely been victimized by it.

As a teenager I worked at a fast-food restaurant. Whenever we took an order, we were required to ask customers if they wanted fries or a drink to go with their order. Initially, I thought: If they wanted fries or a drink, they would have asked for it. Not so. To my surprise, more than half the people I asked changed their order. This technique works on larger purchases as well, from cars to houses. Unfortunately, outside the fast-food world, there is interest involved.

"Would you like a refrigerator to go with that house?"

You've just come to the end of the long and tedious process of qualifying for a home loan. Before the last signature is inked, you are asked, "Do you need any appliances? We could easily add a few luxuries onto that loan. How about a refrigerator?"

What most home buyers don't consider is that this additional purchase goes right on the end of their thirty-year mortgage. Even at a low interest rate like 5 percent, after five years the average cost for a $1,000 refrigerator is nearly double the sales price. And Americans wonder where their money goes.

WHAT KIND OF FOOL?

The poor and the uneducated are particularly susceptible to interest schemes. That's one of the reasons they stay poor. Back when I worked at an advertising agency, we had a client who rented out electronic appliances. You've likely seen similar television commercials: Come to Shams-Rent-to-Own, where you can have it today!

As I was listing the weekly price of a VCR for a television commercial, something didn't look right. I called the store manager.

"This price couldn't be right," I said. "It says $19.99 a week for this VCR."

"No, that's right."

"Twenty dollars a week? For how long?"

"A year."

"You're kidding me. That adds up to more than a thousand dollars for this VCR. It couldn't have cost more than a hundred dollars."

"Actually, we got it for sixty."

"What kind of fool pays more than a thousand dollars for a sixty-dollar VCR?" I asked.

"People who can't wait."

Successful nest eggers are emotionally intelligent. They can wait—even when it's not the easiest course of action. Because of my belief in the Five Lessons, my wife and I decided before we were married that we would never go into debt. We found the engagement ring and the diamond we wanted, but I didn't have enough money to pay for it.

Believe me, I was sorely tempted to break my rule and go into debt. I had other pressures besides the jeweler. To start, a beautiful fiancée whom I wanted to impress—not to mention a future father-in-law who was certain that I was going to keep his daughter barefoot and pregnant. But with my fiancée's support, we held fast to the rule. We put down money to hold the diamond, then had a cubic zirconium set into the ring. No one knew the difference except us. A few months later, I paid off the diamond and we swapped the stones.

For the successful nest egger, freedom and power are infinitely better than momentary satisfaction.

The Millionaire Mentality Does Not Equate Spending with Happiness

> The externals are simply so many props; everything we need is within us.
>
> —ETTY HILLESUM

A friend of mine had an especially hard morning at work and found herself running to the store at her lunch hour. "I bought a five-hundred-dollar dress that I didn't even want." She said, "It just somehow made me feel better."

Like my friend, too many women have adopted shopping as catharsis. "Shopping is therapy," says a television commercial. "Money can buy happiness—just don't pay retail." Equating spending with happiness is the first step to financial self-destruction. Recently, I met a woman whose daughter was working three jobs trying to keep up with her $50,000 credit card debt.

"What did she spend all that money on?" I asked.

"Stuff. Clothes and stuff. She had a bad marriage and she's just trying to fill the void. Unfortunately, all she does now is work."

COMPULSIVE SPENDING

Compulsive behaviors are the cause of many financial disasters. I remember signing copies of *The Five Lessons* at a bookstore in Las Vegas and hearing story after story of lives and nest eggs squandered by people with compulsive gambling habits. The same is true of compulsive spending.

A friend of mine has a client who has spent hundreds of thousands of dollars in purchases she doesn't value or use. Her home is cluttered with stacks of unopened boxes and department store sacks with price tags still attached. It's gotten so bad that she cannot sleep in her own bed because it's covered with junk. She's not really shopping for anything except the "high" that comes from shopping.

Another friend of mine divorced his wife after she refused to get help for her shopping problem, before she could "spend him into oblivion." As he helped her pack her belongings he found, among other things, three identical Chanel purses, still in their boxes with their hefty price tags still attached.

While these examples are extreme, they are demonstrative of the power of this addiction. Compulsive spending is still not listed by the American Psychiatric Association as a distinct disorder, but some experts believe it might soon be. Compulsive spending follows the same pattern of other addictive cycles. With the compulsive spender, the purchase of something creates a temporary psychological "high." Then, after the high dissipates (and it always does), the addict finds herself dealing with the aftermath of her choices, usually a combination of negative emotions: guilt, fear, and shame. The addict, now suffering from this painful "low," naturally seeks relief. So she goes shopping again to create a new high, establishing a powerful and dangerous cycle.

One of the distinct problems with this form of addiction is the lack of negative social consequence. While a drunk is shunned, looked down on, or thrown in jail, the compulsive spender is praised and adored by salespeople, thanked by the recipients of their gifts, and even extolled by the president of the United States for doing their patriotic duty by spending.

Of course, compulsive shopping is not just a women's issue, and some research suggests that compulsive shopping is on the rise among men. Still, it is my experience that this problem is more often a woman's addiction of choice. If you find yourself purchasing things you don't need just for the thrill of buying, or if you knowingly buy things you can't afford, you might need help.

Note: To find help with this problem contact a mental health professional or a shopping addiction support group, or go online for more information and support.

Good News

Remember, just because you have compulsive tendencies doesn't mean you're doomed to financial failure. In fact, the opposite is true: your weakness may become your greatest asset. Remember what Heather wrote in the foreword about changing her behavior? She took her compulsive shopping habits, redirected them to purchasing precious metals instead of junk, and in a relatively short time created a healthy nest egg.

The successful nest egger fosters gratitude as a strategy against materialism and unhappiness.

The best things in life aren't things.

—Ann Landers

One of the great cures for consumption is found in the character trait of gratitude. We live in a world of abundance. The things that bring the greatest joy are not reserved for the wealthy alone. The simplest of pleasures can bring the greatest happiness. What price can we put on inner peace? Or health? Or friendship or love?

Those who forget to be grateful for what they have often waste their lives and wealth looking for more. Their thirst becomes unquenchable as they seek to buy what cannot be bought. It doesn't matter if these people have one dollar or a billion, because they will never have contentment or happiness. They may be in a high tax bracket, but they will never be truly wealthy.

The Millionaire Mentality Protects the Nest Egg

There was a time when a fool and his money were soon parted, but now it happens to everybody.

—ADLAI E. STEVENSON

Successful nest eggers do not risk what they cannot afford to lose. This applies to both investing and living. High-risk, get-rich-quick schemes and other forms of gambling do not appeal to them.

AN EASY TOUCH

When I surveyed my female readers about what they felt was their biggest financial weakness, the number one answer was *being an easy touch.*

Angela [not her real name] was widowed at a young age. With three small children this could have been a financial nightmare. However, her husband had insurance and invest-ments and left her a significant amount of money.

About five years after her husband's death, Angela remar-ried. She was happy for companionship and madly in love. Her new husband, a real estate developer, convinced her not only to invest all her money in his business but to mortgage her house (which was paid off) as well. Less than two years into the marriage not only had he lost all of her money, but she caught him cheating on her. They divorced, leaving Angela emotionally and financially broken and living in near poverty with her children.

Most women (and men) want to be trusting. They want to believe in a happy ending and that the person they love will look out for their best interest. Women need to acknowledge that while this mind-set is a beautiful hope, it is also a poten-tial danger and they should put appropriate safeguards in place.

I didn't mean to hurt you . . .

Wise behavior is not a matter of trust, it's a matter of *wisdom*. That "significant other" who might lose all your money might actually have your best interest at heart. It doesn't matter. Throughout my financial history I have lost more money to people who meant me well than to people who meant me harm. In other words, more financial harm has come from *friends* than from *enemies.* Your spouse may be the kindest, most loving and trustworthy person on the planet. But it doesn't mean that he can protect your assets. Good people lose money every day.

Angela should have decided what she could afford to lose before she put her money and her children's future at risk. Before she remarried, Angela should have transferred the home and much of her assets into a trust for her children, guaranteeing that they would always be taken care of.

PROPER INSURANCE

Insurance has been around for a long time. In fact, insurance existed around 3,000 BC in China. It was later used in ancient Babylon and by the Phoenicians, Hindus, and Greeks. Purchasing the proper amount of insurance is an important financial issue.*

My parents didn't believe in insurance. Early in their marriage they had purchased a policy that didn't pay out when they needed it, and they decided that insurance was just a scam. That's why when my father broke his legs, he didn't have insurance.

Even with all the pain I had experienced growing up with-

---

* For more tips on purchasing the right amount and type of insurance, go to www.thefivelessons.com and click on INSURANCE.

out insurance, my first year of marriage I followed my parents' example. Fortunately my wife, Keri, felt differently. She found an inexpensive health insurance policy for university students and applied for it. Three weeks after she did I was rushed to the hospital for an emergency appendectomy. The cost of the surgery would have put us deep in debt. Thankfully, due to my wife's wisdom, we were spared much pain.

SUCCESSFUL WEALTH BUILDERS PURCHASE PROPER INSURANCE TO PROTECT THEIR GROWING WEALTH.

A study conducted by a Harvard Law School professor found that medical bills and other financial effects of illness or injury contributed to nearly half of the personal bankruptcy filings in the United States. Having proper insurance can make the difference between financial peace of mind and catastrophe.

SUCCESSFUL WEALTH BUILDERS ASK THEMSELVES, "IS THE PERSON I'M TRUSTING WITH MY WEALTH SUFFICIENTLY SKILLED TO HANDLE MY MONEY?"

In *The Richest Man in Babylon,* George S. Clason tells the story of a man who entrusts his hard-earned money to his friend, a bricklayer, to purchase precious gems. Of course, the bricklayer knows nothing about precious gems, and he returns with worthless pieces of glass. "Trust bricklayers with advice about bricks," says his mentor.

Be especially careful with your money when it comes to family. This is what I call the Brother-in-law Syndrome.

As your wealth grows, you will be set upon by others (usually in-laws, it seems) to fund their schemes and business ventures. They will often use emotional manipulation to get you to part with your money. Be kind and simply say, "Let's take your plan to an expert in the field." In most cases, this will end the inquiry. It's not easy to say no to a loved one. But seeing them lose your money is worse. Much worse. And in the end no one is happy.

BURNT TOAST SYNDROME

> The finest inheritance you can give a child is to allow it
> to make its own way, completely on its own feet.
>
> —ISADORA DUNCAN

One of the most destructive of all female financial behaviors is what I call Burnt Toast Syndrome. The first time I shared this discovery with a group of women I was surprised at how affected they were. In fact, they were speechless. A few of them started crying. Afterward I asked how many of them were victims of Burnt Toast Syndrome. Every hand in the room shot up.

This is how I explain Burnt Toast Syndrome. You're making breakfast for your family, and there's enough bread for only one piece of toast per person. You accidentally burn one of them. Who takes the burnt piece?

The answer women usually give is "me." The same holds true for their finances. Even though women live longer than men and need more retirement money set aside, most simply don't do it. Which is why the average income for a woman over sixty-five is less than $7,000 a year. One of the reasons for this disturbing trend is that others gradually and quietly "steal" their retirement from them. Children and other relatives often prey on women (mothers, aunts, grandmothers) to part with very real future needs for those relatives' immediate selfish wants. It's the daughter who "needs" an expensive prom dress or the son who "needs" that $200 pair of basketball shoes. In the moment it often seems easier to just give in and surrender your future funds. Some women thrive on the attention they receive as a benefactor. "They don't steal from me, I'm happy to give it away," one woman said foolishly, trying to convince herself that she was doing good.

One man I know, from a wealthy family, has learned to play his mother like a violin. At the age of thirty (and with several children) he's never held a job for more than a few months. His mother is disappointed with his habits but is unwilling to let her grandchildren suffer. She's a reluctant enabler and continues to do great harm to both her son and her grandchildren.

Let me be clear: *this is absolutely wrong.* It's wrong on two levels. First, it is never okay to give up a need for someone else's wants. Never. You can try to rationalize it, but it is just plain stupidity. Second, the lessons taught to the recipient are remarkably damaging. How would you feel if you discovered that your children were stealing from an elderly widow's pension to buy themselves concert tickets? Or conned a woman down the street out of her Social Security check so they could buy a motorcycle? Obviously you would be disgusted. But that's exactly what you are doing when you give up that future income for their wants. Those who practice this kind of "giving" are practicing a kind of financial suicide *and* raising children to be selfish and entitled. They are creating pathetic, weak people who, unable to stand on their own feet, will continue to prey on others their entire lives. As Clementine Paddleford wrote, "Never put a wishbone, daughter, where a backbone ought to be."

If you're not willing to do what is right because it's right for you, then do it because it's right for your children.

* * *

In the end, whether you *win in the margins* through creating extra income or through savings, both will get you to where you want to be. But serious wealth accumulators employ both to help them reach their goals.

LESSON FOUR

Win in the Margins

LESSON FIVE

Give Back

What I spent, is gone;
What I kept, I lost;
But what I gave away
will be mine forever.

—ETHEL PERCY ANDRUS

Ultimately, the most honorable and enjoyable use of money is in serving others. Freely giving of our wealth is also the only way to fully protect ourselves from our wealth. Yes, money is a powerful ally, but it can also be a spiritual and emotional enemy. While money is an inescapable part of life, it's not life. If money becomes what you live for, you will eventually conclude that life is not worth living.

When you cease {to give}, you begin to die.

—ELEANOR ROOSEVELT

LIFE'S BALANCE SHEET

I was signing books at a bookstore when I noticed a young woman in line who was clearly very excited to meet me. When it was her turn to approach my table she could barely constrain herself.

"Mr. Evans," she exclaimed. "I've wanted to meet you my entire life!"

Flattered, I replied, "So you like my books?"

"Never read them," she quickly replied.

I looked at her with amusement. "Then why did you want to meet me?"

A big smile crossed her face. "I'm one of your Christmas Box House kids."

Her words hit me with great force. "How are you?" I asked.

"I'm great," she replied. She put her arm around the blond teenage boy standing next to her. "This is my brother, Eric," she said. "My caseworker told me that if it wasn't for you we probably would not have been adopted into the same family. I've always wanted to thank you for my brother."

I asked if she wanted to help me sign books, and for the next hour we drank slushies and talked about life.

Success in life cannot be measured on a balance sheet. I believe that the truest measure of achievement is the degree to which we've learned to love. And service, through sharing our wealth and our time, is love made visible.

> In helping others, we shall help ourselves, for whatever good we give out completes the circle and comes back to us.
>
> —FLORA EDWARDS

FINANCIAL KARMA

While generosity feeds the soul, ironically it also feeds the pocketbook. I believe that we receive as we give. It is written in the Bible:

> Will a man rob God? Yet ye have robbed me. But ye say, Wherein have we robbed thee? In tithes and offerings. . . . Prove me now herewith . . . if I will not open you the windows of heaven, and pour you out a blessing, that there shall not be room enough to receive it.
>
> —Malachi 2:8–10

While I don't believe that this promise written in the Bible applies solely to financial blessings, I believe there are karmic principles attached to wealth. We get back when we give. As such, it's important to give not just after we've achieved wealth, but as part of the process.

I have tithed 10 percent of my income since I was eight years old, and in spite of the hardships my family has sometimes faced, I have never felt the loss of this money. Rather, I have felt specifically blessed for my contributions.

On one occasion when my business was doing poorly, I called my accountant and asked him to review my financial records over the past year to see if I had, in fact, paid a true tithe of 10 percent. He called back the next day and told me that I was $800 short. I wrote a check immediately and sent it off. The next day I had three calls from former clients needing work done immediately. Coincidence? Maybe. But I don't think so. I've heard similar stories from friends and associates of different faiths around the world.

The Sin of the Desert Is Knowing Where the Water Is and Not Telling Anyone.

I've always believed that one woman's success can only help another woman's success.

—Gloria Vanderbilt

In addition to sharing your wealth, you have a responsibility to share the lessons of proper money management with others. Within twenty-four hours of reading this book, share this book with a spouse, a child, a girlfriend, or a colleague. Then, as your life improves, share your successes with others. Your example will encourage them to follow your lead. As you share these principles, you will see firsthand the gift of giving back. Teaching the Five Lessons to others will help you internalize them and become better prepared to live and enjoy the fruits of them yourself.

CONCLUSION

Is It Ever Too Late to Start?

A reporter was in my office interviewing me when he noticed the cover of *The Five Lessons* on my desk. He asked me what the book was about. I briefly explained the five principles of wealth, then invited him to attend one of my seminars.

"I could use that," he said, "but I'm afraid it's too late." To my surprise, his eyes welled up with tears. "My daughter called this morning. She needs money for college. I had to tell her that I can't help her. I just don't have it."

Is it ever too late to live these principles? My answer is a resounding "no." Yes, it can be too late to take full advantage of the power of compound interest, but progress is progress. It's never too late to do the right thing or the smart thing and enjoy the benefits it brings.

Hearkening back to my niece's story: just one year into practicing the Five Lessons she was light-years ahead of where she had been and was free of the daily fear and bondage of debt. She and her husband were already enjoying more of the blessings of living in this free and abundant country. Most important, they had hope. And hope is always worth striving for.

IN THE END

We end where we began. Life is not about money. It's about God. It's about love. It's about family and relationships. In sharing with you these principles, it is my hope that you will always give back, that you might find life's true abundance.

All millionaires die, but there are no dead millionaires. Their wealth passes on. As Ray Kroc, the founder of McDonald's, was fond of saying, "I've never seen a Brinks truck following a hearse."

If you have lived successfully, your estate will consist of more than material possessions, and your legacy will be more than a ledger sheet. Remember this: you may use your wealth wisely, find true abundance, and live, as Mark Twain said, "so that even the undertaker mourns your passing."

In the end, this is true wealth.

LESSON ONE

Decide to Be Wealthy

LESSON TWO

Take Responsibility for Your Money

LESSON THREE

Keep a Portion of Everything You Earn

Win in the Margins

Give Back

The Five Lessons

Resources

Glossary and Financial Terms

Winning in the Margins with Extra Income

Winning in the Margins with Savings

Forms

GLOSSARY OF FINANCIAL TERMS

adjustable-rate mortgage (ARM): A mortgage whose interest varies and features predetermined adjustments of the loan interest rate at regular intervals based on an established formula. ARMs typically start with an artificially low interest rate that gradually increases over time. The rise and fall of ARM interest rates generally follow overall interest rate levels.

adjusted cost basis: Adjusted cost basis is used by the IRS for capital gains taxes to determine profit or loss when selling an asset. In selling an investment such as a mutual fund, cost basis is the original investment, plus any reinvested money. In the case of a home, it is the original purchase price, plus the cost of expenditures and improvements that increase property value.

adjusted gross income (AGI): Taxable income (including wages, salaries, and tips) and taxable interest, minus allowable adjustments.

alternative minimum tax (AMT): A federal tax system that ensures that high-earning individuals, estates, trusts, and corporations pay more than they otherwise might. AMT is used to prevent large deductions by the wealthy to assure a minimal level of income tax.

American Stock Exchange (AMEX): The third highest volume of trading in the United States. Trading on AMEX typically consists of index options and shares of small- to medium-size companies.

annuity: An insurance-based contract that provides future payments at regular intervals in exchange for current premiums. A fixed annuity guarantees fixed payments with a constant rate of return. A variable annuity's value fluctuates with that of the assets that are backing it. Annuities allow money to compound and grow without being taxed until withdrawal.

asset allocation: The process of proportioning money between high-risk and low-risk investments.

audit: An audit is used to examine the accounting and financial documents of an individual or a company. It is commonly used by the IRS to determine the accuracy of a tax return.

bankruptcy: A legal action used by an individual or company who is unable to repay debts. The declaration of bankruptcy puts a halt on creditor collection actions.

bear market: A period during which the stock market experiences a strong downturn and usually loses more than 20 percent of its value.

beneficiaries: In the event of death, the people and/or organizations who are left the assets of the deceased.

blue-chip stock: The stock of the largest and most profitable corporations.

bond: A debt instrument issued by a company, city, or state, or the United States government, with a promise to pay regular interest and return on the principal at maturity.

bond yield: The amount a bond will yield is determined by the creditworthiness of the bond's issuer and the maturity date of the bond. Bonds with a high rating are lower risk and thus yield less, while riskier bonds have the potential to yield much more. A bond yield is quoted as the annual percentage rate of return that will be produced if the bond makes its interest payments.

broker: A middleman or agent who is paid commission for taking buy or sell orders for customers.

bull market: A period, usually driven by a strong economy, during which the stock market experiences a strong upward trend.

callable bond: Bonds that are redeemable by the lender prior to a predetermined maturity date. These bonds are held at higher risk due to the high likelihood that if interest rates are lowered, the holder will have her investment returned early, thereby possibly creating the need to reinvest funds at a lower interest rate.

capital gain: When a capital asset such as a stock is sold at a higher price than the investor's purchasing price. This is a way an investor can grow her financial portfolio. When such an asset is sold below cost it is defined as a capital loss.

capital gains distribution: Distribution to shareholders of a mutual fund or a real estate investment trust (REIT), through which profits are gained by the selling of stocks or bonds. Shareholders are subject to capital gains taxes on profits.

cash value insurance: A type of insurance that results in high commissions for insurance salespeople. This insurance carries an investment feature as well as a death benefit.

certificate of deposit (CD): Created by banks, this investment pays interest at either a fixed or a variable rate. If sold directly by a bank, the principal will be returned upon maturity, subject only to penalties for early withdrawal. If sold through a broker, principal value may vary, as with bonds, and cashing in early can result in a lower principal than the amount invested. CDs are generally not recommended for those in higher tax brackets, as interest paid is fully taxable.

commercial paper: Unsecured short-term promissory notes issued by banks and corporations which are usually due in 2 to 270 days. These promissory notes are generally safe and flexible, and are a major component of money-market fund investment portfolios. Proceeds from commercial paper must be used to finance current operating expenses.

commission: The fee paid to a real estate agent or broker for executing the sale of a home or other investment. This compensation may be a percentage of the sale price or simply a fee charged to clients for buying and selling futures and futures options contracts.

commodity: Goods or items of trade or commerce, such as food, metal, or other physical substances that investors buy or sell, usually on the futures market. A commodity is also a financial instrument (derivative) whose value is established through an intangible security, such as a treasury bill or stock.

common stock: Securities that represent equity ownership in a company, giving the investor not only a vote on such matters as the direction of the company but also a share in the company's profits, through dividend payments or capital appreciation. It must be noted that the amount of dividend sharing a company disperses is at the discretion of its management, and that the failure of such company may result in the loss of investment.

comparable market analysis (CMA): A study completed by those in the real estate industry comparing homes of similar value recently placed on the housing market and/or sold in any given area.

consumer debt: Loan balances on goods and/or services that depreciate in value immediately or over time, generally leaving one paying high interest rates on products no longer useful or of adequate significance.

consumer price index (CPI): Published every month by the United States Department of Labor, the CPI measures the pace of U.S. inflation by compiling data through tracking the prices of consumer goods and services as they increase or decrease during a given period.

credit report: A report that tracks a person's credit history, helping lenders determine whether to extend a loan.

debit card: A card that looks like (and has the convenience of) a credit card but, instead of creating consumer debt, enables the holder to charge purchases against funds in her already established checking account.

debt metabolism: The phenomenon in which people tend to maintain a certain level of debt regardless of external circumstances.

deductible: The out-of-pocket cost that must be personally paid when filing an insurance claim.

deduction: An expense that may be subtracted from one's taxable income when filing taxes.

derivative: An investment whose value is derived in part from the value and characteristics of another underlying security.

discount broker: A broker who generally offers no investment advice and who either has commission rates substantially lower than the norm or is on full salary.

diversification: The practice of putting money in different kinds of investments in order to minimize risk or to improve overall portfolio performance.

dividend: Compensation (most often quarterly) paid to a company's existing shareholders from its stock profits.

Dow Jones Industrial Average (DJIA): The Dow, as it is called, contains thirty stocks that trade on the New York Stock Exchange. This is the best known U.S. index of stocks and is a barometer of how shares of the largest U.S. companies are performing.

down payment: The non-financed portion of a house's purchase price, which a home buyer pays up front in cash.

equity: A synonym for *stock.* Also used in the real estate world, referring to the difference between the market value of a home and what is owed on it.

estate: The total assets of an individual, minus loans and liabilities, at time of death.

estate planning: The often twofold process of structuring one's assets to minimize estate taxes upon death, and determining how those assets will be distributed.

financial asset: A property or investment having value that could be monetarily realized upon liquidation of that property or investment.

financial liabilities: Outstanding debts.

financial planner: Individuals who help establish financial plans for their clients. Financial planners come from many different backgrounds and hold various degrees, so it is important to note that although a financial planner may have licenses and designations (such as CFP and ChFC) to indicate their extent of expertise, they are not required by law to license.

fixed-rate mortgage: A mortgage whose interest rate (and therefore house payment) will not change during its fifteen- to thirty-year life (term).

401(k) plan: Offered to employees by for-profit companies, this type of retirement savings plan is usually exempt from federal and state income taxes, allowing it to compound over time.

403(b) plan: Much like a 401(k), but offered to employees of nonprofit organizations.

full-service broker: A broker who generally charges the highest commission rates while providing investment research and advice, as well as the services involved in purchasing and selling securities. Full-service brokers may also advocate investment strategies that will financially benefit them.

future: Usually representing a short-term gamble on the short-term direction of the price of a commodity, a future carries the obligation to buy or sell a commodity or security on a specific day for a preset price.

guaranteed-investment contracts (GICs): A pure investment product which often appeals to conservative investors, because one usually knows a year in advance what their interest rate will be in the coming year, therefore eliminating worry over fluctuations to one's investment. GICs, however, generally carry a low interest rate comparable to a short-term certificate of deposit.

home equity: See *equity.*

home equity loan: A loan (sometimes called a line of credit) under which a property owner uses her residence as collateral and can then draw funds up to a prearranged amount against the property.

index: (1) A security market index measures the performance of a specific type of security, creating a statistical composite. (2) The overall level of interest rates that a lender uses as a reference to determine the interest rate of an individual adjustable-rate loan.

individual retirement account (IRA): A retirement account that may be established by an individual who is employed or receiving alimony. IRA contributions are tax deductible and profits made in the account are tax deferred. The IRS limits the annual amount of deductible contributions that may be made to this account.

inflation: The gradual decline of purchasing power of the dollar, creating rising prices, usually related directly to increases in the money supply created by the federal government.

initial public offering (IPO): A company's first sale of stock to the public. Securities offered in an IPO are typically those of emergent companies seeking to expand more rapidly and needing outside equity capital to support growth.

interest rate: The amount a debtor must pay a creditor for the use of their money. As a general rule, the riskier the loan, the higher the rate of interest.

junk bond: A bond with a speculative credit rating of BB (Standard & Poor's) or Ba (Moody's) or lower. These bonds offer investors higher yields than those of financially sound companies, but are also, of course, more risky.

Keogh plan: A tax-deferred pension account designated for those who work for unincorporated businesses or are self-employed.

leverage: Refers to the practice of disproportionally controlling a large sum of money with a small amount of cash invested. Through leveraging one can borrow a substantial amount (sometimes up to 50 percent) of a stock price and use all the funds (both the initial investment and the borrowed amount). Repayment of this margin loan is made through selling the stock. A large return can be earned if stock prices move favorably. However, losses can also be substantial, relative to the margin, if stock prices decline.

limited partnership (LP): A business or investment with both general and limited partners. General partners are responsible for the management of the business and are liable for the total obligations of the partnership. Limited partners have limited liability, while providing capital and sharing in investment returns—which are often also limited due to high commissions and management fees.

load: Commission deducted from investment money, which is paid to brokers who sell commission-based mutual funds.

market capitalization: The total dollar value of the outstanding stock of a company. This dollar value is computed by multiplying the price per share by the number of shares outstanding.

Moody's ratings: A rating system which measures the default risks of various bonds. The following ratings system, from highest to lowest, is used: Aaa, Aa, A, Baa, Ba, B, Caa, Ca, C.

mortgage broker: A fee-based company or individual who matches borrowers and lenders, while handling the necessary details for borrowers to obtain loans against real property.

mortgage life insurance: A life insurance policy that pays off the remaining balance of the insured person's mortgage upon death.

mortgage-backed bond (GNMAs and FNMAs): The Government National Mortgage Association (GNMA or Ginnie Mae) passes the principal and interest payments of borrowers to its investors. Thus, when a homeowner makes a mortgage payment, after subtracting a small service fee, GNMA forwards the mortgage payment back to its investors. The Federal National Mortgage Association (FNMA or Fannie Mae) is a government-sponsored corporation that is publicly owned. Mainly working with mortgages backed by the Federal Housing Administration, it purchases mortgages from lenders and resells them to investors.

municipal bond: Offered to state or local governments by investors, these bonds are usually tax-free and are used to pay for special projects such as highways, museums, and parks.

mutual fund: Investment capital (made up of stocks, bonds, or other securities) that is pooled by people who share common investment goals and managed by an investment company.

National Association of Securities Dealers Automated Quotation (NASDAQ) system: An electronic network that allows people from all over the country to trade from their offices, constantly updated by real-time prices that appear on their computer screens.

negative amortization: In amortization, monthly payments are large enough to pay the interest and reduce the principal of a mortgage. When a loan repayment schedule has an outstanding principal balance that increases, rather than decreases, the unpaid interest is added to the outstanding balance and results in negative amortization. (This may occur when a cap is placed on a monthly mortgage payment but not on the interest rate.) This means that even after making several payments, a person may actually owe more than she did at the beginning of the loan.

net asset value (NAV): The per-share value of your fund's investments. Also referred to as share price, meaning the dollar value of one share.

New York Stock Exchange (NYSE): In terms of total volume and value of shares traded, the NYSE is the largest stock exchange in the world.

no-load mutual fund: An open-end investment company, which does not have fees or commission payments attached to it.

open-end mutual fund: A fund that does not generally limit the number of its shares or investors. Some open-end funds do eventually close to new investors, but existing shareholders can usually continue to buy as many shares as they desire from the company.

option: A contract that affords the right to buy or sell shares of a common stock at a predetermined price on or before its stipulated expiration date.

payday loans (Also called cash advance or payday advance loans): Short-term loans intended to help borrowers get by until the next payday. While there are laws regulating how much interest can be charged by financial institutions, these businesses get around these laws by charging "fees" rather than "interest." These fees are typically 15 percent of the loan.

pension: A benefit offered by some companies, pension plans pay a monthly retirement income based on years of service with an employer.

preferred stock: Although this type of stock does not ordinarily carry voting rights, it does give the holder prior claim over common stockholders on earnings and assets if the company is ever liquidated.

price/earnings (P/E) ratio: Used extensively in stock analysis statistics (as it assists investors in understanding how relatively expensive a stock price is), the P/E is determined by the current price of a stock divided by the current earnings per share of the issuing company.

prime rate: The interest rate at which banks lend to their most creditworthy corporate customers. Most banks charge a few points above prime on mortgages and other personal loans.

principal: Usually relating to the initial balance borrowed on a loan, it can also refer to the amount originally placed in an investment.

prospectus: A legal disclosure document that is extremely useful in making an informed investment decision concerning a company. It describes products and services, past performance, proposed business plans for the future, and risks of investing, as well as fees and other applicable information.

real estate investment trust (REIT): The mutual fund of real estate investments, these trusts invest in a collection of properties and trade on the major stock exchanges.

refinance: A change in debt obligation, usually by taking out a new mortgage loan at a lower interest rate, to pay off an existing mortgage that was held at a higher interest rate.

return on investment: The percentage of profit made on an investment.

reverse mortgage: A mortgage agreement that enables elderly homeowners to borrow against their home's equity without selling or having to move. Homeowners typically receive monthly tax-free payments until the total principal and interest reaches its equity limit, at which point the lender either gets repaid in full or acquires the house.

Russell 2000: An index that charts the profits of two thousand smaller U.S. company stocks.

Securities and Exchange Commission (SEC): The federal agency that enforces U.S. securities laws while regulating and monitoring investment companies, brokers, and financial advisers.

simplified employee pension individual retirement account (SEP-IRA): Often used by the self-employed, SEP-IRAs are quite easy to establish and, over the years, allow annual pretax contributions to compound.

Social Security: Financed by the Social Security tax, this insurance is given to retired or disabled individuals (with disabilities expected to last at least one year) to compensate for lost wages.

Standard & Poor's (S&P) ratings: A rating system that measures the default risks of various bonds. The following ratings system, from highest to lowest, is used: AAA, AA, A, BBB, BB, B, CCC, CC, C.

Standard & Poor's 500 index: An index which evaluates the performance of five hundred U.S. large-company stocks, whose total market value accounts for roughly 80 percent of all stocks traded in the United States.

stock: An investment that buys ownership in a corporation in exchange for a portion of that corporation's earnings and assets (although not all stocks pay dividends). One can also make money investing in stocks through appreciation in the price of the stock.

10/10 rule of debt retirement: Diverting 10 percent of your income to paying off debt and 10 percent to building a nest egg. This technique of debt repayment is primarily done for psychological reasons.

term life insurance: An insurance contract without an investment or cash buildup component, which offers a death benefit. The premium remains constant for a specific number of years, at which time the policy is usually renewable.

treasury bill: An IOU from the federal government that matures within a year.

treasury note: An IOU from the federal government that matures within one to ten years.

treasury bond: An IOU from the federal government that matures in more than ten years.

underwriting: The process of exposing the risks inherent in granting a particular loan (or insurance) and establishing suitable terms and conditions for the loan (or insurance).

will: A legal document asserting the wishes of the deceased concerning her minor children and the distribution of her assets after death.

Wilshire 5000: Tracking closer to six thousand companies, this index serves as a good standard when investing, as it measures the rise and fall of stock in corporations big and small on the major U.S. stock exchanges.

winning in the margins: A process in which successful wealth builders find additional ways to add to their growing wealth accumulation.

zero-coupon bond: Bonds that do not pay explicit interest prior to the loan's maturity and are not shielded with tax breaks. An investor receives one payment, in which interest has been accruing and compounding semiannually at the rate of original interest to maturity.

WINNING IN THE MARGINS
WITH EXTRA INCOME

Remember, winning in the margins with extra income will come through paying attention to the unique opportunities that already surround you.

JOBS TO INCREASE YOUR INCOME

* Wait tables on weekends.
* Turn your hobbies into jobs.
* Learn to make jewelry and sell it at local fairs.
* Teach cooking classes.
* Referee.
* Teach piano lessons.
* Babysit.
* House-sit.
* Clean houses or office buildings.
* Refurbish furniture and sell it to consignment stores.
* Pick up a paper route.
* Repair cars.
* Put up and take down other peoples' Christmas lights.

* Do freelance work.
* Start a lawn-care business.
* Donate plasma.
* Help coach a local sporting team.
* Become a massage therapist.
* Teach private swim lessons.
* Sell homemade rolls or treats around the holidays.
* Sell gift baskets.
* Get certified and teach aerobics or water aerobics.
* If you are good at photography, start a small business.
* Breed animals.
* Teach language lessons.
* Look into credible home-based business opportunities.

For a free online report on how you can increase your earning ability, visit my Web site at www.winninginthemargins .com and enter "win" when asked for your passkey.

WINNING IN THE MARGINS
WITH SAVINGS

When winning in the margins with savings, always remember to apply the four mind-sets.

1. The Millionaire Mentality carefully considers each expenditure.
2. The Millionaire Mentality believes that freedom and power are better than momentary pleasure.
3. The Millionaire Mentality does not equate spending with happiness.
4. The Millionaire Mentality protects the nest egg.

As you fill out your monthly Cash Flow form, review each expenditure, then begin looking for ways to save. Remember that the Internet has put more power in consumers' hands than ever before. Be sure to take full advantage of it. In each applicable category we have included a list of Web sites to help you save.

Don't expect all of the suggestions to be right for you. Check off the ones that you find helpful. Remember: the goal is to reduce your expenditures by an additional 10 percent of your income so as to double your contribution to your nest egg.

BUILDING THE NEST EGG

* Put a minimum of 10 percent of your monthly salary and 75 to 100 percent of extra income into your nest egg.
* If you receive a pay increase, put the extra away in savings.
* Take advantage of banks' and brokerage firms' automatic-withdrawal plans that will take money from your checking account and put it into your savings account.
* When you have finished paying off your debt, divert the money you were using to pay it off into your nest egg.
* Collect all your spare change in a jar; when it is full, deposit it into your nest egg. It will add up to more than you think. In our research, a cup of miscellaneous coins is worth about $24.

MORTGAGE AND RENT

* You can save thousands of dollars in interest charges by shopping for the lowest rate. Always obtain more than one quote before accepting a loan. Be sure to ask about all fees involved.

* Use an adjustable-rate mortgage (ARM) only if you can't afford a fixed-rate loan or if you intend to sell the home within a few years.
* Choose the shortest-term loan you can afford.
* Be cautious in taking out home equity loans. The loans reduce or may even eliminate the equity that you have built up in your home. (Equity is the cash you would have if you sold your house and paid off your mortgage loans.)
* By making just one extra mortgage payment every year you can reduce the time span of the loan by up to seven years. Plan, right now, to double your payment one month this year or to split the amount of thirteen payments into twelve even payments.
* Check the tax assessment of your property. If you think you are paying taxes based on too high an evaluation, contact the assessor's office and file an appeal. According to the International Association of Assessing Officers, over half of all appeals result in the reduction of taxes.
* Look into refinancing your mortgage anytime rates fall a half percentage below your existing rate.
* Drop private mortgage insurance (PMI) if it is no longer necessary. While this insurance is sometimes required when you first purchase a home, in most cases it can be dropped after you have paid off 20 percent of the loan. Ask your lender about termination rules. It may have been

done automatically, but if not you could save an extra $25 a month.

* Rent out a room or basement.
* Find a roommate.
* Rent from a private party rather than a corporation when possible—you may avoid automatic periodic increases in rent.
* Spend no more than 25 percent of your monthly gross income on your rent. The extra money you allocate for rent in a slightly more upscale complex means less money for your other expenses: utilities, loan payments, entertainment, food, and, most important, savings.

FOOD

* Shop with a list. Plan your shopping based on sales and specials and avoid impulse purchasing.
* Comparison shop by looking at the unit price listed on the shelf below each item. The unit price indicates the cost per pound or ounce.
* Join a wholesale superstore such as Costco or Sam's Club; buy necessities such as some food staples and toiletries in bulk.
* Eat out more frugally and avoid beverages; many restaurants make a large profit on beverages, especially alcohol.

Few people check the price of drinks, and restaurateurs know this. On one occasion I found that a simple soda cost nearly as much as some of a particular restaurant's entrées.

* Ordering vegetarian meals saves money, as they generally cost less than meat-based entrées.

* Try brown-bagging it twice a week instead of eating out. Some consumer groups estimate that this will save you at least $500 per year. (Not to mention the calories.)

* Do your grocery shopping on double coupon days.

* Purchase generic brands. According to some experts, this can save you an average of 40 percent off your annual grocery bill.

* Watch for discounts on nonperishables that you buy regularly and stock up when they are on sale.

* Shop for meat early or late in the day, when certain cuts may be at a discount.

* Prepackaged goods cost more. Cook from scratch more often.

* Always keep the ingredients for at least one quick-and-easy meal in the house to avoid unplanned eating out when tired or in a hurry.

* Always check receipts for accuracy, especially with coupons and produce.

* Check prices on grocery store sales. Actual savings may be insignificant or misleading.

* Buy loss leaders. These are the items on the front page of the ad and are often sold at cost just to get you into the store.

* Fresh-food areas usually have a section featuring items that will expire within a few days. These items can be discounted anywhere from 50 to 70 percent.

* Avoid purchasing nongrocery products, such as cosmetics and household items, in grocery stores. These products are usually marked up 25 percent higher than they are in discount drugstores.

* Grow your own garden.

* Search the Internet for freebies and coupons from manufacturers. (See list at the end of this section.)

* Have a potluck or barbecue dinner with friends instead of going out to dinner.

* You've heard it before: never shop hungry. Researchers have shown that, on the average, consumers spend 10 percent more when they go to the grocery store hungry.

* Carry a calculator with you whenever you shop.

* Do your grocery shopping on Monday. Prices on average are lower.

* The best all-purpose cleaner is chlorine bleach. You can clean toilets, sinks, floors, and walls and potentially save $20 a month.

FOOD SAVINGS WEB SITES:

* coupons.com
* q-pon.com
* hotcoupons.com
* coolsavings.com
* couponcart.com
* couponorganizer.com
* frugalshopper.com
* valpak.com

UTILITIES

* Check windows and doors for air leaks. Use caulk to seal them. A package of caulk will cost less than $5. Check your local home-improvement stores for more ideas.
* Insulate your water heater. Although your water heater and pipes may be insulated on the inside, they can lose heat and energy through the outside casing. Insulating blankets are available at most home-improvement stores. They are easy to install and can save you up to 3 percent on monthly heating bills.
* Turn down your heat by five degrees and wear a sweater. This could save 15 percent on your heating bills. During the summer months, use the air conditioner as little as

possible. You will see dramatic savings in your electric bill.

* Contact your energy supplier. Your local electric and gas companies may have various reduced-rate plans depending on your age, income level, or dwelling.

* Replace 100-watt bulbs with 60-watt bulbs.

* Sometimes the best way to save money takes money. Replacing old appliances with newer and more energy-efficient ones may save you money in the long run.

* Install a water-flow regulator in showerheads and toilet bowls. This can reduce the amount of water use by 50 percent without a noticeable difference in pressure.

* Buy energy-saving lightbulbs.

* Unplug appliances.

* Fix leaky faucets. Leaky faucets can waste six to ten gallons of water per day.

* Install dimmer switches in living areas such as dining rooms and bedrooms. Lights dimmed 15 percent reduce energy consumption by 15 percent.

* Use electric timers to conserve energy. These can be purchased at any home-improvement store.

* Use a programmable thermostat to lower the heat at night after you're asleep. Also, lower your heat when you're not home.

* Pay for a year's worth of cable or satellite television or Internet. This may help you avoid extra monthly charges.

* Use high-energy appliances such as dishwashers and washing machines on off-peak hours. Call your utility company to find out about different rates for on- and off-peak times.
* Close heat vents in any room that does not need to be heated.
* Attics should be insulated to prevent heat or air-conditioning from escaping.
* Double-pane your windows.
* Renting to own is likely the most expensive way to purchase something (such as the VCR I mentioned earlier). If you can't wait, find another way to finance the item you want to buy.
* Be aware of your phone usage. Calls made after 5 P.M. are cheaper in most places than calls placed between 8 A.M. and 5 P.M.
* Shop around for a calling plan that best fits your needs.
* Turn off lights, television, and other appliances when leaving a room.
* Learn to fix minor things around the house to avoid having to pay a plumber or handyman.
* Check your utility bill. One study showed that four out of five companies overcharged on their utilities. Utilities' auditing companies report that on the average most homeowners are overcharged by 20 percent.

TRANSPORTATION:
CAR PAYMENTS AND EXPENSES

* When buying a new car, check out car guides to help you with model information and pricing.
* Don't buy more car (or cars) than you need. Most of my millionaire friends drive economy cars.
* Before you buy a used car, compare the seller's asking price with the average retail price in a blue book. Try www .kellybluebook.com.
* Have a mechanic you trust inspect the car before you agree to purchase.
* Always think long-term when buying a car. You pay much more than the initial cost of the car, including gas, insurance, registration fees, maintenance, and repairs.
* Buy regular unleaded gas. Many studies have shown that more expensive fuel isn't worth it. (Check with your dealer or mechanic.)
* Fill up on gas when shopping at a warehouse wholesaler where gas is cheaper.
* Carpooling with coworkers twice a week could save you up to $20 a month.
* Buy commuter passes where available.
* Service cars regularly, before problems develop. Change the oil in your car (yourself) every three thousand miles. Keep wheels aligned and balanced.

* If a mechanic finds a problem during routine maintenance, get a second opinion and another estimate before making repairs.
* Don't buy tires that are said to last thousands of miles longer than you intend to drive your car. It is a lot more expensive and unnecessary.
* By paying cash, you can save a nickel per gallon at many gas pumps.
* Use air-conditioning in your car only when needed. The extra load on the engine severely reduces mileage.
* Avoid poor driving habits. Maintaining a constant speed over a long distance saves gas. Excess braking wastes fuel up to 20 percent.
* An interesting Web site to check local gas prices is www .gasbuddy.com.
* A friend of mine figured out a way to drive cars for free. In fact, he actually made money on them. Every six months or so he'd go to local car auctions and buy a car. He'd drive the car for six months, then turn around and sell it at a profit. He'd then go back to the auction and start the process all over again.

AIR TRAVEL

* Fly on Sundays rather than Saturdays.
* Book flights early; most flights increase in cost when you book less than two weeks in advance.
* Be flexible when booking flights.
* Buy tickets during the week. Oftentimes fares are raised temporarily for the weekend.
* Ask about discounts for seniors and children.
* Be sure to check on discount carriers.

Web Sites for Hotel, Travel, and Airfare Discounts

* expedia.com
* hotels.com
* cheapfares.com
* 11thhourvacation.com
* hotwire.com
* havekids-willtravel.com. This site offers a fascinating guide to family travel anywhere in the world at remarkably reduced rates—oftentimes free.

AUTOMOBILE INSURANCE

* Always shop around to get the best possible insurance rates. A study by Progressive Insurance shows that the cost of an auto insurance policy for the same driver with the same or comparable coverage can vary from company to company by as much as $1,000 a year.
* Raise your deductible. According to the Insurance Information Institute, raising your deductible from $200 to $500 could reduce your collision and comprehensible cost by 15 to 30 percent.
* Make sure your current policy accurately reflects your needs. It is important to update your information on your driving record, age, and the model of car you drive. The correct information can reduce your rate.
* You may receive added discounts by holding a policy with one company for a long period of time.

MEDICAL INSURANCE

* As suggested in Lesson Four, always have at least minimal medical coverage to protect yourself and your nest egg against catastrophe.
* Always get second opinions before making major medical decisions.
* If you spend time in a hospital, carefully check the item-

ized bill to be sure that there were no incorrect charges. One consumer-advocacy group reports that 90 percent of hospital bills contain errors, with overcharges accounting for approximately two-thirds of those errors.

* Buy generic drugs and no-frills vitamins. You can save up to 50 percent on some drugs. (Always check with your doctor before taking generic drugs.) Shop around for prescriptions on the Internet or use a mail-order company. The average savings are 30 percent.

HOMEOWNER'S INSURANCE

* Make your home more resistant to disaster. (Find out how through your insurance agent or a company representative.)
* When deciding how much insurance to buy, don't include the value of the land under your home, as it isn't at risk for theft or fire.
* Install smoke detectors, dead-bolt locks, and burglar alarms to cut your premiums. (Ask your insurance agent if you qualify for any discounts.)
* Review the value of your possessions yearly to be sure you're paying only for coverage you need. (This should already be on your Net Worth form.)
* If you are paying homeowner's insurance through the government, look into private insurance, as it may be cheaper.

DEBT PAYMENTS

* Use credit cards that don't charge an annual fee, such as Discover, AFBA Industrial Bank, or USAA Federal Savings.
* Refinance your mortgage for a lower interest rate and use that money to pay off existing debt.
* Keep the two credit cards with the lowest interest rates.
* When paying monthly credit card bills, pay the full amount or calculate how much you can afford to pay over the minimum.
* When applicable (see Lesson Three) use some of your savings to get out of debt.
* Seek help through a nonprofit consumer credit counseling service, or seek out a financial support group.
* Resolve that you will use your credit cards only for essentials over the next six months.

CLOTHING

* Shop clearance sales. (When stores begin to put out next season's clothes you can save 30 to 75 percent on your family's clothing budget.)
* Avoid clothes that must be dry-cleaned. Buy machine-washable clothes rather than silks or wools.
* Hand wash and iron your shirts instead of dry-cleaning them.

* Shop at thrift stores or upscale clothing consignment stores.
* Shop for children's school clothes after school starts to avoid the rush and peak prices.
* Minimize accessories that won't be used frequently.
* Stick with classic styles and don't always change your wardrobe to suit current fashion trends.
* Shop for only a few hours at a time—you'll be less likely to buy impulsively.

CLOTHING AND HOME ACCESSORIES WEB SITES

* bluefly.com
* overstock.com
* jumpondeals.com
* justdeals.com
* gogoshoppers.com
* smartbargains.com

Forms

THE FIVE LESSONS

NET WORTH SHEET

AS OF _____
Date

ASSETS Current Liquid Assets		**OTHER LIABILITIES** Current Liabilities	
Cash (on hand)	$ _____	Charge Account	$ _____
Checking Account	$ _____	Credit Cards	$ _____
Savings Account	$ _____	Insurance Due	$ _____
Certificates	$ _____	Taxes Due	$ _____
Money Owed You	$ _____	Current Bills Due	$ _____
Tax Refund Due	$ _____	Line of Credit	$ _____
Life Insurance (cash value)	$ _____	Other _____	$ _____
Stocks/Bonds	$ _____	Other _____	$ _____
Mutual Fund Shares	$ _____	Other _____	$ _____
Precious Metals	$ _____	Other _____	$ _____
Other _____	$ _____	**Total Current Liabilities**	$ _____
Other _____	$ _____		
Total Current Assets	$ _____	**LONG-TERM LIABILITIES**	

FIXED ASSETS

		Auto Loan #1	$ _____
		Auto Loan #2	$ _____
Home	$ _____	Installment Loan	$ _____
Automobiles	$ _____	Personal Loan	$ _____
Furniture	$ _____	Mortgage Loan	$ _____
Jewelry	$ _____	Other _____	$ _____
Personal Property	$ _____	**Total Long-Term Liabilities**	$ _____
Other _____	$ _____		
Total Fixed Assets	$ _____	**TOTAL LIABILITIES**	$ _____

DEFERRED ASSETS

Retirement Plan	$ _____
IRA	$ _____
Other _____	$ _____
Other _____	$ _____
Total Deferred Assets	$ _____

Total Assets	$ _____
Total Liabilities	$ _____
NET WORTH	$ _____

TOTAL ASSETS $ _____

THE FIVE LESSONS

NET WORTH SHEET

AS OF _____
Date

ASSETS Current Liquid Assets		**OTHER LIABILITIES** Current Liabilities	
Cash (on hand)	$ _____	Charge Account	$ _____
Checking Account	$ _____	Credit Cards	$ _____
Savings Account	$ _____	Insurance Due	$ _____
Certificates	$ _____	Taxes Due	$ _____
Money Owed You	$ _____	Current Bills Due	$ _____
Tax Refund Due	$ _____	Line of Credit	$ _____
Life Insurance (cash value)	$ _____	Other _____	$ _____
Stocks/Bonds	$ _____	Other _____	$ _____
Mutual Fund Shares	$ _____	Other _____	$ _____
Precious Metals	$ _____	Other _____	$ _____
Other _____	$ _____	**Total Current Liabilities**	$ _____
Other _____	$ _____		
Total Current Assets	$ _____	**LONG-TERM LIABILITIES**	
		Auto Loan #1	$ _____
FIXED ASSETS		Auto Loan #2	$ _____
Home	$ _____	Installment Loan	$ _____
Automobiles	$ _____	Personal Loan	$ _____
Furniture	$ _____	Mortgage Loan	$ _____
Jewelry	$ _____	Other _____	$ _____
Personal Property	$ _____	**Total Long-Term Liabilities**	$ _____
Other _____	$ _____		
Total Fixed Assets	$ _____	**TOTAL LIABILITIES**	$ _____

DEFERRED ASSETS

Retirement Plan	$ _____
IRA	$ _____
Other _____	$ _____
Other _____	$ _____
Total Deferred Assets	$ _____

Total Assets	$ _____
Total Liabilities	$ _____
NET WORTH	$ _____

TOTAL ASSETS $ _____

THE FIVE
LESSONS

NET WORTH SHEET

AS OF _____
Date

ASSETS Current Liquid Assets		**OTHER LIABILITIES** Current Liabilities	
Cash (on hand)	$ _____	Charge Account	$ _____
Checking Account	$ _____	Credit Cards	$ _____
Savings Account	$ _____	Insurance Due	$ _____
Certificates	$ _____	Taxes Due	$ _____
Money Owed You	$ _____	Current Bills Due	$ _____
Tax Refund Due	$ _____	Line of Credit	$ _____
Life Insurance (cash value)	$ _____	Other _____	$ _____
Stocks/Bonds	$ _____	Other _____	$ _____
Mutual Fund Shares	$ _____	Other _____	$ _____
Precious Metals	$ _____	Other _____	$ _____
Other _____	$ _____	**Total Current Liabilities**	$ _____
Other _____	$ _____		
Total Current Assets	$ _____	**LONG-TERM LIABILITIES**	

FIXED ASSETS

		Auto Loan #1	$ _____
		Auto Loan #2	$ _____
Home	$ _____	Installment Loan	$ _____
Automobiles	$ _____	Personal Loan	$ _____
Furniture	$ _____	Mortgage Loan	$ _____
Jewelry	$ _____	Other _____	$ _____
Personal Property	$ _____	**Total Long-Term Liabilities**	$ _____
Other _____	$ _____		
Total Fixed Assets	$ _____	**TOTAL LIABILITIES**	$ _____

DEFERRED ASSETS

Retirement Plan	$ _____
IRA	$ _____
Other _____	$ _____
Other _____	$ _____
Total Deferred Assets	$ _____

Total Assets	$ _____
Total Liabilities	$ _____
NET WORTH	$ _____

TOTAL ASSETS $ _____

THE FIVE LESSONS

NET WORTH SHEET

AS OF _____
Date

ASSETS Current Liquid Assets		**OTHER LIABILITIES** Current Liabilities	
Cash (on hand)	$ _____	Charge Account	$ _____
Checking Account	$ _____	Credit Cards	$ _____
Savings Account	$ _____	Insurance Due	$ _____
Certificates	$ _____	Taxes Due	$ _____
Money Owed You	$ _____	Current Bills Due	$ _____
Tax Refund Due	$ _____	Line of Credit	$ _____
Life Insurance (cash value)	$ _____	Other _____	$ _____
Stocks/Bonds	$ _____	Other _____	$ _____
Mutual Fund Shares	$ _____	Other _____	$ _____
Precious Metals	$ _____	Other _____	$ _____
Other _____	$ _____	**Total Current Liabilities**	$ _____
Other _____	$ _____		
Total Current Assets	$ _____	**LONG-TERM LIABILITIES**	

FIXED ASSETS

		Auto Loan #1	$ _____
		Auto Loan #2	$ _____
Home	$ _____	Installment Loan	$ _____
Automobiles	$ _____	Personal Loan	$ _____
Furniture	$ _____	Mortgage Loan	$ _____
Jewelry	$ _____	Other _____	$ _____
Personal Property	$ _____		
Other _____	$ _____	**Total Long-Term Liabilities**	$ _____
Total Fixed Assets	$ _____	**TOTAL LIABILITIES**	$ _____

DEFERRED ASSETS

Retirement Plan	$ _____	**Total Assets**	$ _____
IRA	$ _____	**Total Liabilities**	$ _____
Other _____	$ _____	**NET WORTH**	$ _____
Other _____	$ _____		
Total Deferred Assets	$ _____		

TOTAL ASSETS $ _____

For free copies of this form, visit our Web site at www.thefivelessons.com.

THE FIVE LESSONS

CASH FLOW SHEET

CASH FLOW FOR _____
Date

INCOME	Planned	Actual
Salary 1 (after taxes)	$ _____	$ _____
Salary 2 (after taxes)	$ _____	$ _____
Other Income	$ _____	$ _____
Other Income	$ _____	$ _____
Total Income	$ _____	$ _____

EXPENDITURES		
Nest Egg (*min. 10% of total income*)	$ _____	$ _____
Charitable Donations	$ _____	$ _____
Mortgage or Rent	$ _____	$ _____
Food	$ _____	$ _____
Utilities	$ _____	$ _____
Auto Payments	$ _____	$ _____
Misc. Auto Expenses	$ _____	$ _____
Repair	$ _____	$ _____
Maintenance	$ _____	$ _____
Gas	$ _____	$ _____
Auto Insurance	$ _____	$ _____
Life Insurance	$ _____	$ _____
Homeowner's Insurance	$ _____	$ _____
Medical Insurance	$ _____	$ _____
Clothing	$ _____	$ _____
Debt Payments	$ _____	$ _____
Misc. Expenses	$ _____	$ _____

TOTAL EXPENDITURES	$ _____	$ _____
Income Less Expenditures	$ _____	$ _____

For free copies of this form, visit our Web site at www.thefivelessons.com.

CASH FLOW SHEET

THE FIVE
LESSONS

CASH FLOW FOR _____
Date

INCOME	Planned	Actual
Salary 1 (after taxes)	$ _____	$ _____
Salary 2 (after taxes)	$ _____	$ _____
Other Income	$ _____	$ _____
Other Income	$ _____	$ _____
Total Income	$ _____	$ _____

EXPENDITURES

	Planned	Actual
Nest Egg *(min. 10% of total income)*	$ _____	$ _____
Charitable Donations	$ _____	$ _____
Mortgage or Rent	$ _____	$ _____
Food	$ _____	$ _____
Utilities	$ _____	$ _____
Auto Payments	$ _____	$ _____
Misc. Auto Expenses	$ _____	$ _____
Repair	$ _____	$ _____
Maintenance	$ _____	$ _____
Gas	$ _____	$ _____
Auto Insurance	$ _____	$ _____
Life Insurance	$ _____	$ _____
Homeowner's Insurance	$ _____	$ _____
Medical Insurance	$ _____	$ _____
Clothing	$ _____	$ _____
Debt Payments	$ _____	$ _____
Misc. Expenses	$ _____	$ _____
TOTAL EXPENDITURES	$ _____	$ _____
Income Less Expenditures	$ _____	$ _____

For free copies of this form, visit our Web site at www.thefivelessons.com.

CASH FLOW SHEET

THE FIVE
LESSONS

CASH FLOW FOR _____

Date

INCOME	Planned	Actual
Salary 1 (after taxes)	$ _____	$ _____
Salary 2 (after taxes)	$ _____	$ _____
Other Income	$ _____	$ _____
Other Income	$ _____	$ _____
Total Income	$ _____	$ _____

EXPENDITURES		
Nest Egg (*min. 10% of total income*)	$ _____	$ _____
Charitable Donations	$ _____	$ _____
Mortgage or Rent	$ _____	$ _____
Food	$ _____	$ _____
Utilities	$ _____	$ _____
Auto Payments	$ _____	$ _____
Misc. Auto Expenses	$ _____	$ _____
Repair	$ _____	$ _____
Maintenance	$ _____	$ _____
Gas	$ _____	$ _____
Auto Insurance	$ _____	$ _____
Life Insurance	$ _____	$ _____
Homeowner's Insurance	$ _____	$ _____
Medical Insurance	$ _____	$ _____
Clothing	$ _____	$ _____
Debt Payments	$ _____	$ _____
Misc. Expenses	$ _____	$ _____
TOTAL EXPENDITURES	$ _____	$ _____
Income Less Expenditures	$ _____	$ _____

CASH FLOW SHEET

THE FIVE
LESSONS

CASH FLOW FOR _____
Date

INCOME	Planned	Actual
Salary 1 (after taxes)	$ _____	$ _____
Salary 2 (after taxes)	$ _____	$ _____
Other Income	$ _____	$ _____
Other Income	$ _____	$ _____
Total Income	$ _____	$ _____

EXPENDITURES		
Nest Egg *(min. 10% of total income)*	$ _____	$ _____
Charitable Donations	$ _____	$ _____
Mortgage or Rent	$ _____	$ _____
Food	$ _____	$ _____
Utilities	$ _____	$ _____
Auto Payments	$ _____	$ _____
Misc. Auto Expenses	$ _____	$ _____
Repair	$ _____	$ _____
Maintenance	$ _____	$ _____
Gas	$ _____	$ _____
Auto Insurance	$ _____	$ _____
Life Insurance	$ _____	$ _____
Homeowner's Insurance	$ _____	$ _____
Medical Insurance	$ _____	$ _____
Clothing	$ _____	$ _____
Debt Payments	$ _____	$ _____
Misc. Expenses	$ _____	$ _____

TOTAL EXPENDITURES	$ _____	$ _____
Income Less Expenditures	$ _____	$ _____

JOIN THE FIVE LESSONS REVOLUTION

A Note from Richard Paul Evans

Dear Reader,

I have an idea. A big idea. But before I share it with you, I want you to take a minute and seriously consider this question:

What Kind of a World Would We Live in if Only the Bad People Had Money?

It would be a dark world indeed. There would be no parks or museums. Schools and churches would shut down and hospitals would help only the elite few. Most of us would be enslaved, if not with physical chains then with financial ones. With this in mind, I'll share my idea—or maybe I should say *dream.*

Over the past twenty years I've seen the power of the Five Lessons change people's lives: not only financially but emotionally, mentally, and spiritually as well. I've seen my wonderful readers "Give Back" by reaching out and helping one another to succeed. I wish that more *good* people had wealth. This has led me to my dream. I dream of creating a community of One Million **Compassionate** Millionaires. Wealthy people who use their power to improve their lives, their communities, and the world around them.

We're accomplishing this dream with an online wealth club called **The Five Lessons Institute** that provides powerful weekly mentoring, teleclasses, monthly and weekly plans of action, and powerful tools to aid you in your wealth accumulation. As a member of this community, you'll be able to share with other members and watch your wealth grow and the community's wealth grow. We'll do it together. Imagine being one of a million people around the globe following the same success strategy. We have already established relationships with scores of major retailers who offer special discounts to our community. Talk about strength in numbers. While others are treading financial waters, we'll be swimming ahead to success.

Obviously it will be expensive to run this institute, but by spreading the cost out over the whole community you'll receive thousands of dollars of benefits for very little. The price to join the Five Lessons Wealth Club is very low—just $10 to join and $9.95 a month per family. And because we believe in *giving back*, part of that will go directly to charity.

Incredible idea, isn't it? And timely. If the economy is the *Titanic,* this is a lifeboat. But this plan is helpful not only right now, in a time of economic crisis, but also in times of prosperity when we can really build wealth. If this sounds great to you, you're not alone. Already thousands have joined us. If you're ready to join our community then go to 5Lessons .com and sign up online. And welcome to the revolution!

ABOUT THE AUTHOR

RICHARD PAUL EVANS is the author of thirteen *New York Times* bestselling novels and five children's books. He has won the American Mothers' Book Award, the 2005 Romantic Times Reviewers' Choice Award for women's fiction, and two first-place Storytelling World Awards for his children's books. His books have been translated into more than eighteen languages. More than fourteen million copies of his books are in print worldwide. *Newsweek* and *The Washington Post* have noted his business savvy. At the age of thirty, Evans was the recipient of the Ernst & Young Entrepreneur of the Year Lifetime Achievement Award.

He is also the founder of the Christmas Box International, an organization dedicated to helping abused and neglected children. More than sixteen thousand children have been housed in Christmas Box Houses. He is the recipient of the *Washington Times* Humanitarian of the Century Award and the Volunteers of America National Empathy Award. He lives in Salt Lake City, Utah, with his wife and their five children.

Please send e-mail correspondence to:

Richard@thefivelessonsinstitute.com

Please send mail to:

Richard Paul Evans
P.O. Box 1416
Salt Lake City, Utah 84110

Printed in the United States
By Bookmasters